THE ULTIMATE HOCKEY DRILL BOOK

VOLUME 1

RICHARD TRIMBLE

MASTERS PRESS

A Division of Howard W. Sams & Co.

Published by Masters Press
A Division of Howard W. Sams & Company
2647 Waterfront Pkwy E. Dr, Suite 100, Indianapolis, IN 46214

97 98 99 00 01 02   10 9 8 7 6 5 4 3 2 1

Trimble, Richard M.
    The ultimate hockey drill book / Richard M. Trimble.
        p.   cm.
    Contents: v. 1. Beginning skills.
    ISBN 1-57028-133-5 (v. 1 : pbk.)
    1. Hockey--Coaching.   I. Title.
GV848.25.T75 1997   97-20413
796.962'2--dc21   CIP

Participation in the game of ice hockey is by its very nature dangerous, so drills need to be properly supervised, taught and demonstrated. Coaches must always be cognizant of potential hazards, including flying pucks, hard checks and the ability levels of players relevant to the difficulty of drills being called for. Neither the author or the publisher of this book accept responsibility for any injuries incurred during the execution of any drill described herein.

CONTENTS

To Andy

INTRODUCTION

This book came into being largely due to my faulty memory. In every sport that I coach, I have always been fascinated by drills, coaching devices and teaching gimmicks. Whenever I visited a practice or a camp, I had a notepad with me to jot down drills and coaching points. Whenever I worked a camp I asked the visiting coaches what some of their favorite drills were and oftentimes they provided me with loose-leaf binders and spiral notebooks of their own. Books and coaching seminars also added to my collection, of course.

The result was a vast and continually growing eclectic accumulation of drills for players of all levels of ability. Then I began to find myself in a rut. Each coach will inevitably settle into a pattern of using his or her favorite drills in their practices. If the drills are effective then there is really nothing wrong with this trend. However, a certain staleness will have emerged and this could translate into tedium for both the coach and the players. I had "forgotten" many of my drills. Therefore, I found myself scouring my own notebook for "new" drills. Realizing a compulsive need for better organization of my data, this book came into existence.

It is my fondest hope that you can add some of these drills to your collection.

Coach Richard "Rick" Trimble
June,1996

A PHILOSOPHY OF DRILLS

Every drill must have a specific intent. As obvious as that seems, it is often overlooked. The coach must ask himself what he hopes to impart to his players through the drill about to be executed. Is the intention skill enhancement, instruction, agility, or conditioning? Having discerned this, considerations then range into the duration of the drill, timing of the drill in practice, amount of ice surface needed, and equipment to be used. The tempo of the drill should be considered, too.

For instance, if the drill is purely instructional, then it falls into a low-tempo mode and it may only be employed once. An agility drill should not last longer than five to seven seconds in duration or it falls into the conditioning category. A conditioning drill should be high tempo and most often should be placed at the end of practice. On a cautionary note, conditioning drills should always relate to specific skills utilized in the sport that you teach. Why on earth, for example, do hockey coaches insist on punishing recalcitrant players with on-ice pushups? Suicide sprints, board jumps and the like are more grueling and they impart not only the message but a hockey-specific skill, too. Skill enhancement drills can be repetitive and part of a regular practice routine. Furthermore, the tempo will vary in accordance with the age and skill level of the players you are working with. The more advanced they are, the more you can insist on a higher tempo.

This book will be broken down into the aforementioned drill orientations: instructional, agility, skill enhancement and conditioning. It is the coach's responsibility to create his drills with a specific philosophy in mind.

It is my firm belief that about 75 percent of what is drilled on the ice can be taught off the ice. Moreover, off-ice drills can definitely be used to enhance, not just impart, on-ice skills.

As a further thought, when designing your drill sequence and practice plan, why not separate drills with drills? In other words, rather than waste precious ice-time by setting up cones and so forth while the players stand around, have them loop the rink in a designated free-skating drill while you are performing your set-up/clean-up chores. Use one such drill per practice and then have the players move on the whistle. It shows organization and it sets an atmosphere of a good work ethic and team hustle. Plus, you have maximized ice-time usage.

When you are "installing" drills, or teaching them for the first time, it can be helpful to use only half of the ice (if the drill allows this) to see that the players get it before working a mirrored replica of the drill to the other side or coming back the other way.

To keep your drills flowing despite misplayed passes or overskated pucks, place a coach with a collection of pucks at a strategically located position on the ice (endzone or neutral zone) to feed players on a drill pattern who have lost their puck.

In short, keep things moving!

PRACTICE ORGANIZATTON

What drill book would be complete without a few thoughts on how best to integrate and utilize the drills explained? It is truly surprising how many coaches do not know how to effectively organize and orchestrate a practice session. With ice hockey being one of the few sports in which the practice time is often a costly affair financially, coaches must come to practice prepared with a definite drill sequence and practice plan.

Conceptually, the coach should break his or her practice time into four components: warm-up, individual skills, combined skills or team work, and conditioning. In the beginning of the season, more work will probably be spent honing individual skills in preparation for the season. As the team runs through the regular game season, then combination work and team work may assume a greater percentage of the practice time. The coach will need to work on things that the team is not doing well or executing to satisfaction. All four components of the practice session will always be present however; the difference lies in what is to be emphasized.

Combination drills such as passing 3-on-0 or 2-on-2 are helpful in the early and preseason as the coach will be looking for effective and workable tandems, lines and player pairings.

During the season, one of the strongest pieces of advice I can offer is also one of the simplest: take notes. I coach both baseball and ice hockey and throughout my career of over 25 years I have always made a notepad as necessary to my coaching attire as my habitual chewing gum. In the heat of a game, you will never remember all of the corrections you need to make, things you want to say and changes you may wish to think about. Write them down. These game notes, often dictated to the team statistician on the bench, will help you compose your practice plan for the next time your team works out. I find that I must even jot down a word to two on the things that I want to mention to my team in between periods or innings. Some coaches save these notes game-to-game and even year-after-year, but I generally discard them after I have made the necessary adjustments and corrections.

Another aspect of the "write it down" philosophy relates to the practice plan itself. Frame out what you want to work on and then commit it to writing. Run copies so that all of your coaches are literally on the same page. This is advice that is as sound for the college coach as it is for the clinic coach. By writing out the plan, you will be able to keep to the time frame allocated. Hockey coaches cannot waste precious ice-time for the financial reasons stated earlier.

Warm-ups and conditioning must be related to the sport. In ice hockey, your pre-practice warm-ups involve skating and stretching rather than static and stationary stretches, although the latter does have its place off the ice. The conditioning phase, always scheduled for the end of practice, must also relate directly to the game of hockey. Sprints with start-and-stop cross-overs, board jumps, positional windsprints and so forth must enhance not only the athlete's physical stamina, but also his or her sport-specific skills.

Think it out, write down, and then teach and drill. Keep your practices focused, efficient and on time. Bring a dry-mark "blackboard" with you so that drills can be diagrammed prior to their execution. Photocopy pages from this book and write in your own time of duration and coaching points, as shown on each page.

It's all here. Now it's up to you to make things work.

KEY

X	Player or Skater
G	Goaltender
C	Center or Coach
F	Forward
D	Defenseman
△	Cone or Pylon
• Ⓧ	Puck Position or Player with the Puck
—Ⓖ—	Fallen Goaltender
⌐	Stick
⌒	Goal
❶ ❷ ❸	First, Second, Third Shot or Pass
🪑	Chair
- - - →	Pass
- · - · →	Shot
—⊤	Stop or Check
∿→	Skating Path or Route
⋀⋀⋀→	Backwards Skating Route

Note that the drills are basically set up in each chapter in an order of difficulty with the easier drills in the beginning of each chapter and proceeding to more difficult ones at the end.

POWERSKATING DRILLS

"To acquire the warrior spirit and, once having acquired it, to conquer or perish with honor is the secret to victory!"

Gen. George S. Patton

NAME OF DRILL: Powerskating Drills I, II, and III
SKILL TO BE TAUGHT/ENHANCED: Skating
DURATION OF DRILL: 2-4 runs[*]

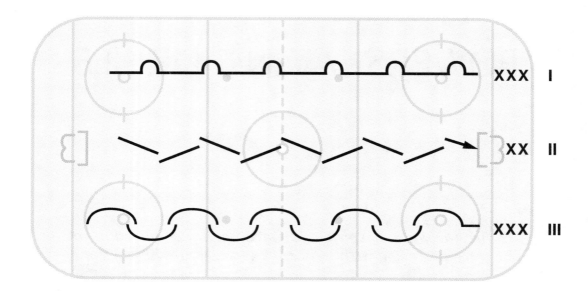

DESCRIPTION OF DRILL:
Line players along one endline and have them work their way up ice using the following sequence of drills:

DRILL I: KNEE FLEXION AND THRUST
Perform deep knee bends and leap upward with powerful thrusts; do this first with both legs simultaneously and then perform with one leg each.
DRILL II: V–SKATE
Place heels about 2 feet apart and and work push and extension; emphasize the knee flexion at about 90 degrees. Leg-thrust should be performed with leg pushing out to full extension.
DRILL III: BARROW CUTS
Cut large circles on inside edge of skate, going up ice with all the player's weight on one skate and alternating. The edge of the blade should be at 45-degree angle to the ice and the radius of each circle should be 7-10', again emphasize the knee flexion.

COACHING POINTS:
If ability levels allow, Drill III, and even Drill I, can be done both forward and backward.

*Each of the powerskating drills, and many of the skating agility drills to follow, are best taught in "runs" up and down the ice rather than a specific time allocation. In most of these drill pages, the time is omitted for coaches to fill in the appropriate number of "runs" based on ability levels, length of practice time, and number of skaters.

NAME OF DRILL: Powerskating Drills IV and V
SKILL TO BE TAUGHT/ENHANCED: Developmental Powerskating Skills
DURATION OF DRILL: 2-4 runs

Drill IV:

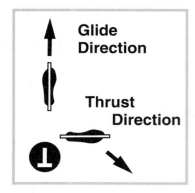

Drill V:

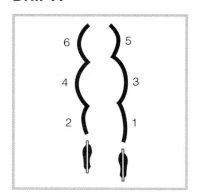

DESCRIPTION OF DRILL:
Two different drills are described here. Both are designed to teach powerskating leg push.

DRILL IV: PUSH–CART DRILL
a. Teach the proper terminology as to which skate is the push leg and which is the glide leg.
b. Align the skater's feet in a "T" position with the glide leg pointed in the direction they wish to go. Have them keep the glide leg's skate on the ice and push only with the push, or thrust, leg all the way up or across the ice.
c. Reverse the push and glide legs to return back to point of origin.
DRILL V: HEEL PUSH
After three good hard strides to get them going, have the skaters keep both skates on the ice and propel themselves by pushing the inside edge and back-half of the blade into the ice. Remember, keep both skates on the ice!

COACHING POINTS:
• Emphasize inside edge pushes in both of these drills as well as knee flexion (90 degrees is optimal) and powerful leg through.
• In Drill IV, the coach should look for the toe of the push leg to be the last part of the blade to leave the ice.

NAME OF DRILL: Powerskating Drills VI and VII
SKILL TO BE TAUGHT/ENHANCED: Edge Control

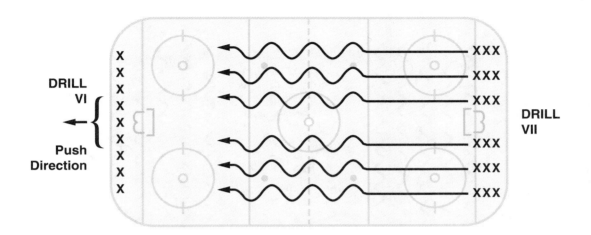

DESCRIPTION OF DRILL:

DRILL VI: MOVE THE WALL

This is a teaching drill for beginning skaters, and it shows them how to apply their inside edges. Use the term "bite into the ice" when teaching this drill. Line your players up along the sideboards of the rink; have them face the boards and align their skates in the "T" formation described earlier. The glide skate should be pointed directly perpendicular to the boards. On the whistle they must push against the boards in an effort "to make the rink bigger." On each whistle they should shift their feet to get the other skateblade to "bite into the ice."

DRILL VII: DRUNKEN SAILOR DRILL

At the risk of being politically incorrect with the name of this drill, it does accurately describe the body movement. After skating from the goalline toward the neutral zone, the players will place all of their body weight on one skate and, in an exaggerated cross-over, high-step the other leg over the down skate. Repeat with other skate. Have the players feel the balance factor as they cross over. Also teach them to feel the outside edge bite into the ice. This drill is good for advanced players, too, but have them take wider arcs when they cross over.

COACHING POINTS:

Drill VII is also good for teaching younger players the cross-over maneuver.

NAME OF DRILL: Powerskating Drills VIII, IX, and X
SKILL TO BE TAUGHT/ENHANCED: Skating

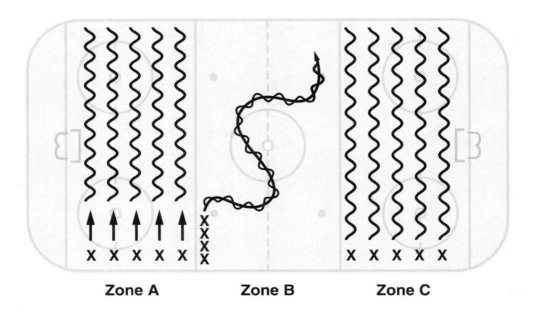

Zone A   **Zone B**   **Zone C**

DESCRIPTION OF DRILL:
Keeping the skates on the ice at all times after initial acceleration, ex-ecute these three maneuvers: (differentiated by zone)

DRILL VIII: ZONE A
Drive off the thrust leg to full extension with the glide leg. Pull the toe of the thrust leg back into a "recovery" position with heels close together by scraping the skate-toe along the ice.
DRILL IX: ZONE B
Execute cross-overs while keeping the skates on the ice.
DRILL X: ZONE C
Carioca: start out, then widen base, cross-under, bend ankle and work edges (push off the cross-under bent ankle)

It is better to perform these drills for the full length of the ice than is shown above, although smaller players can benefit from the series/sta-tions as shown.

COACHING POINTS:
- Emphasize knee flexion.
- Emphasize recovery in Zone A.
- Hand positioning is important, too. As the player drives off his right foot (left skate striding in front), the left hand tucks to the hip with the palm upward, and the right arm drives back, not out to the side. This upright palm technique is emphasized in the Glantz clinics and helps keep the hands tight to the body.

NAME OF DRILL: Powerskating Drills XI, XII, and XIII
SKILL TO BE TAUGHT/ENHANCED: Powerskating

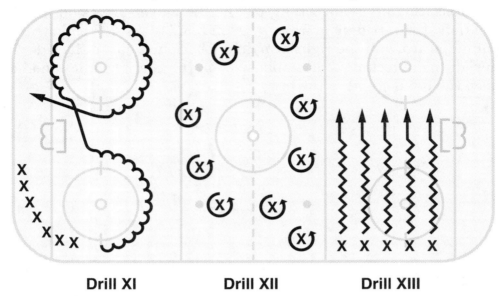

Drill XI   **Drill XII**   **Drill XIII**

DESCRIPTION OF DRILL:

DRILL XI: CIRCLE PUSH–CART DRILL
Replicate the push-cart drill (Drill IV) by keeping the glide skate on the ice and pushing only with the thrust leg. The difference here is that you are emphasizing circle turns and an inward lean, albeit slight. Drive the heel of the push skate into the ice. Perform forward and backward.

DRILL XII: STATIONARY PIVOTS
Keep skate A on the ice and push yourself in a circle by thrusting the skate and toe of boot B. Repeat with other skate.

DRILL XIII: BACKSKATE WITH BOTH SKATES NEVER LEAVING THE ICE
For want of a better name to this drill, the aforementioned describes it. Have the players do exactly that, but emphasize the return of the heels to the "V" position before beginning each outward thrust. Perform slowly and deliberately; "load up" before each thrust.

Stationary Pivots:

COACHING POINTS:
Break the skaters up into five groups and utilize all five circles for Drill XI. Also, Drill XIII is best performed along the full length of the ice.

NAME OF DRILL: Powerskating Drill XIV
SKILL TO BE TAUGHT/ENHANCED: Stride Power on Cross-overs

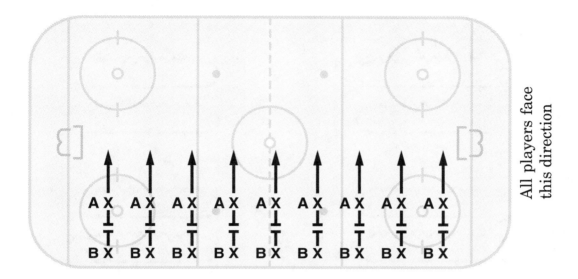

DESCRIPTION OF DRILL:
- Set players up in pairs along one side of rink.
- Player A provides resistance by pushing against player B's shoulder as Player B walks over his skates, performing typical cross-over stride.*

COACHING POINTS:
- Emphasize full extension of the non-stepping-over leg as well as the angle of the skate to the ice (45 degrees) and the outside edge being dug into the ice.
- Be advised that younger players have a lot of difficulty with this drill.

*With players facing in the direction shown in the diagram, they will be stepping their right foot over their left.

NAME OF DRILL: Powerskating Drill XV
SKILL TO BE TAUGHT/ENHANCED: Transition — Foreskate to Backskate

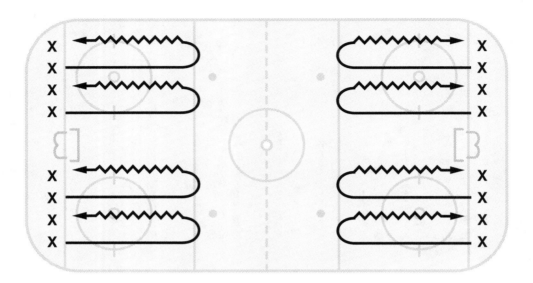

DESCRIPTION OF DRILL:
- Align players at each end of rink.
- On whistle every other player at each goalline will skate (or run on toes from V-start) to blue line.
- At blue line they perform a C-cut turn to backskate rearwards, returning to goalline.
- Upon reaching the goalline, the skater must perform a two-leg backward (snow-plow) stop or a one-leg stop on a designated skate (returning to the T-start position).
- Repeat drill with other half of remaining players.

COACHING POINTS:
- Although this drill is a fairly standard one, the coaches should emphasize the C-cuts, the running stride, and the quick turn.
- Coaches may wish to have skaters return, backskating, by using only one skate in C-cutting. Film studies have shown that many young skaters will only use one skate when they C-cut backward.
- Skaters should all perform their turns in a prescribed direction which will be subsequently reversed by the coach.

NAME OF DRILL: Powerskating Drills XVI, XVII, and XVIII
SKILL TO BE TAUGHT/ENHANCED: Starts, Toe-thrusts, Backskating Agility

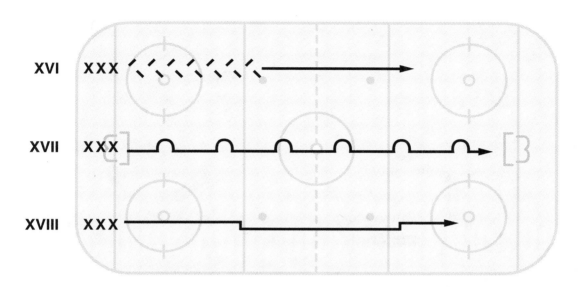

DESCRIPTION OF DRILL:
DRILL XVI: V-START TOE-RUNNING
Have the players balance on their toes (younger players can use the stick as a tripod to help their balance as they await the whistle). Emphasize knee flexion. On the whistle, they sprint to the red line on their toes.
DRILL XVII: BACKSKATING LEAPS
As players backskate, they must sit,thrust and leap. As an alternative, have them hold their stick with both hands at arms length in front at shoulder height. Then they will alternately kick the ends of their sticks, emphasizing balance.
DRILL XVIII: SQUATS
As players skate through the neutral zone, they are to sit down at full squat flexion, literally riding their skates on their haunches. This emphasizes and strengthens knee and hip flexion. It is a good warm-up drill for stretching, too.

COACHING POINTS:
Although the terms T-start and V-start are both used in this text, coaches should teach both concepts since they emphasize different aspects of edge control. The difference is the positioning of the heels and toes.

T-Start :

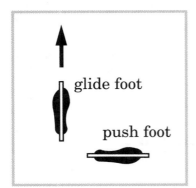

glide foot

push foot

V-Start :

NAME OF DRILL: Powerskating Drills XIX and XX
SKILL TO BE TAUGHT/ENHANCED: Edge Control

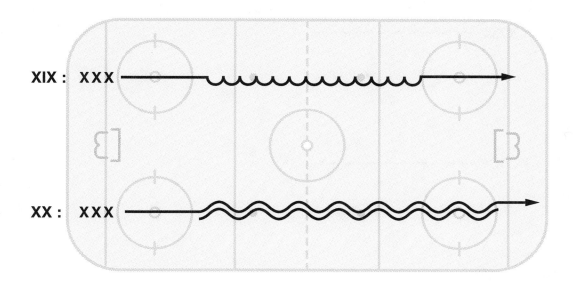

DESCRIPTION OF DRILL:
DRILL XIX:
Similar to the single edge glide-n-push previously described as "barrow cuts," have the players work hard "C-cuts" with one skate only as they propel themselves up the ice, or at least through the neutral zone depending upon skill levels. Repeat with the other skate.
DRILL XX:
Then work up and back using both skates to involve the inside edge of one skate and the outside edge of the other.

COACHING POINTS:
In both drills emphasize knee flexion and the "feel" of digging the skate edge into the ice. With younger players, have then literally "hear" the crunch of the blade into the ice.

NAME OF DRILL: Powerskating Drills XXI and XXII
SKILL TO BE TAUGHT/ENHANCED: Edge Control, Push and Balance

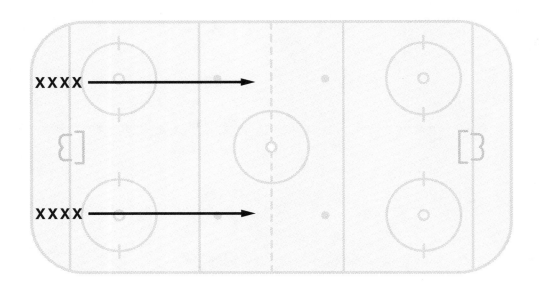

DESCRIPTION OF DRILL:
Line the players up at one end of the ice.

DRILL XXI: RUSSIAN DANCER (variation)

For balance, have the skaters squat down as they proceed through the neutral zone; call for good knee and hip flexion. Then have them throw one leg straight out in front of themselves, thereby skating on one skate. Alternate legs.

DRILL XXII: PROVIDENCE REAR SKATE SNAKE

Named after a drill I saw at PC's summer camp, the notion is to keep the lead skate on the ice and push off the heel of the rear skate in an "S" pattern as shown below. It is a difficult maneuver. Work to accelerate with the push off each edge and emphasize inside/outside. Emphasize the push of the toe, also.

COACHING POINTS:
- Keep both skates on the ice at all times.
- Emphasize ankle flexion on the rear skate.
- Drill XXI, The Russian Dancer (variation) can be executed backskating, too!

NAME OF DRILL: Powerskating Drill XXIII
SKILL TO BE TAUGHT/ENHANCED: Skating Agility, Drive

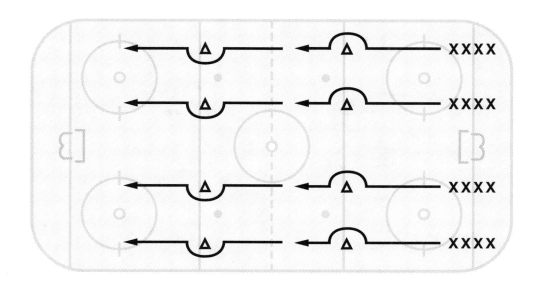

DESCRIPTION OF DRILL:
• Align the players at one end of the ice as shown.
• On the whistle, they will skate toward the cone (or coach) and hop on to either the left skate or the right skate as predetermined.
• Emphasize the hop with good knee flexion and driving on to the inside edge of the landing skate.
• As the players become more proficient, more cones can be added.
• Build up to this drill by having the players slowly and deliberately skate the length of the ice leaping on to the inside edge of the outside skate, alternating feet of course.

NAME OF DRILL: Powerskating Drills XXIV
SKILL TO BE TAUGHT/ENHANCED: Turns, Pivots

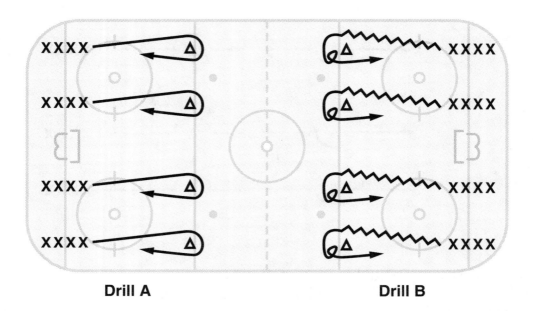

Drill A   **Drill B**

DESCRIPTION OF DRILL:
- Drill A is a simple "hockey turn" or tight-turn drill. Emphasize a slight weight shift on to the heels, a low center of gravity with good knee flexion, inside skate in front and inside shoulder down and in. Have the players execute a cross-over in coming out of the turn to re-accelerate.
- Drill B is more complex. The players will backskate to the cone and then execute a turn-out pivot. Emphasize the heels coming within 6" of each other! Then re-accelerate on the foreskate. Be sure that they are all pivoting to the same side and then work the other side.

NAME OF DRILL: Powerskating Drill XXV Tag-Team Push
SKILL TO BE TAUGHT/ENHANCED: Leg Power, Team Work

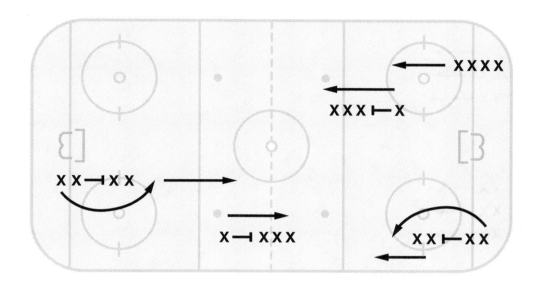

DESCRIPTION OF DRILL:
• Align players in groups of four at one end of the ice as shown.
• On the whistle, the back player will push the other three players who are not allowed to aid the pusher by skating in any manner.
• Once they reach the end of the ice, the pusher assumes the lead position in front of the line and then new rearward person does the pushing.
• Repeat until all four players have pushed the team the length of the ice at least once.
• The drill is diagrammed in various stages of the push-sequence.

COACHING POINTS:
Definitely include the goalies in this drill. You may even elect to have them be primary pushers for an intrasquad competition.

NAME OF DRILL: 2-Man Drills: Powerskating XXVI
SKILL TO BE TAUGHT/ENHANCED: Powerskating, Strength, Edge
Control

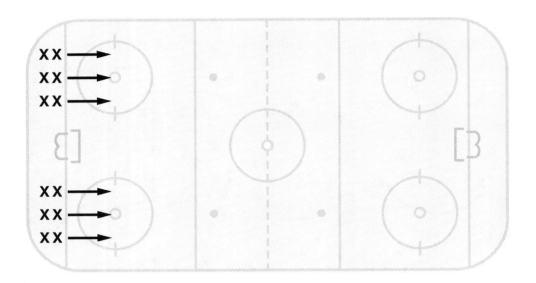

DESCRIPTION OF DRILL:
Align players, in pairs of approximately equal size, along one goalline.

PUSH–PUSH DRILL:
Each player has one hand on his stick and one on partners; each tries to
pull or push opponent off balance; this can also be done with each player
having hands on one stick in a cross-checking position. One stick may be
used in a take-away mode.
CHOO–CHOO TRAIN:
Players will line up facing far end of rink and they will grip the ends of
each others sticks; player in front skates forward while player behind
offers minimal resistance through snow-plowing; switch positions upon
reaching end of rink; can be done forward and backward.

COACHING POINTS:
- Be sure the players work to dig their edges in.
- Be careful not to slip into face of partner when performing the Choo-choo Train drill since the players are close to each other; some coaches have a player pull the other who is lying down on the ice. This is NOT recommended for safety reasons.
- Alignments in the drills are as follows:

Push-Pull:

Choo-choo:

- In the backskating resistance drill, do not allow the players to cross-under accelerate; have them "cut C's" all the way.

NAME OF DRILL: Powerskating Drill XXVII: Rubber Band
SKILL TO BE TAUGHT/ENHANCED: Stride Power

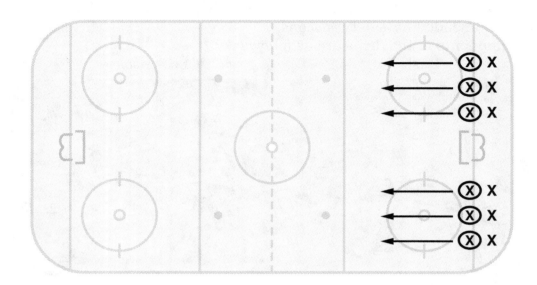

DESCRIPTION OF DRILL:
- Pick up bicycle tire inner tubes from a local bike shop.
- Pair players in combinations of two about equal size and stature.
- One player skates with tube around waist and another player, trailing, provides moderate resistance.
- Switch players for return trip.
- Use old, blown tubes — the dealer will probably be happy to fish them out of the trash and you will save money!

COACHING POINTS:
- Front skater should work on digging edges into ice.
- This drill has been done with players skating backward, but it can be dangerous this way and is to be discouraged.
- Trailing player should grip tube with both hands.

SKATING AGILITY DRILLS

"If you want to be a good coach, you'd better be a great actor!"

Coach Fred Shero

NAME OF DRILL: Stick Drills
SKILL TO BE TAUGHT/ENHANCED: Skating Agility

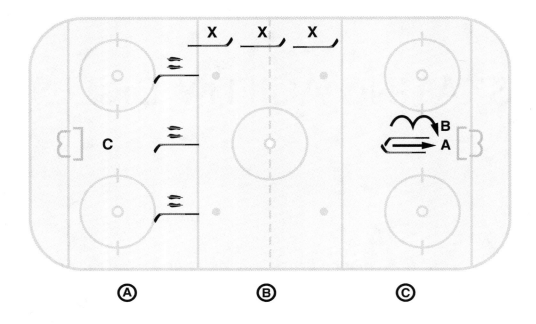

Ⓐ Ⓑ Ⓒ

DESCRIPTION OF DRILL:
DRILL A:
Facing the coach, players will leap over their sticks, as the sticks are lying on the ice, with both feet simultaneously or with one foot. The latter emphasizes stopping by digging the middle of the blade into the ice. This drill is good for goalies, too. Emphasize foot speed and quickness.
DRILL B:
Facing one end of the rink, players will cross-over to "jump-start" their way across the ice. This emphasizes the cross-over start to attain a powerful, quick stride.
DRILL C:
A difficult drill, two sticks are placed on the ice in a parallel manner. The skater places one skate in between the sticks (A). He or she is to keep that skate straight while the other skate (B) performs C-cuts skating backward. Emphasize the initial toe thrust in boot B and knee flexion for both legs. Note that this drill is for backskating, so the player in the diagram would be facing the net.

NAME OF DRILL: More Stick Drills!
SKILL TO BE TAUGHT/ENHANCED: Powerskating and Agility

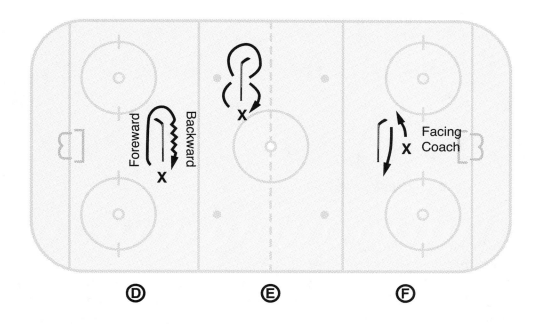

DESCRIPTION OF DRILL:
Drill D:
With stick lying on the ice, have the players skate forward along one side, pivot with a tight radius and backskate along other side. Pivot again and repeat. Emphasize close heel placement for the pivots.
Drill E:
With stick lying on the ice, players will perform figure 8's by stepping over the stick and employing tight turns. This can be done backwards, too, although carefully.
Drill F:
With the stick lying on the ice, have the players attempt to leap, with good knee-flexion thrust, from one one of the stick to the other. They will land on one skate. They will need to really push and leap sideways for distance and width. This is a good off-ice drill, too.

COACHING POINTS:
Stick drills A and F should also emphasize the stopping component in powerskating.

NAME OF DRILL: Airplane Stick Drills
SKILL TO BE TAUGHT/ENHANCED: Cross-overs/Cross-unders, Balance

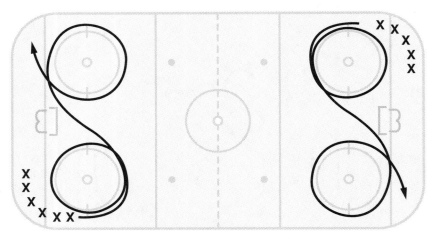

Zone I   Zone II

DESCRIPTION OF DRILL:
- Align players in the corners as shown.
- Skaters in Zone I will execute a figure-8 turn series of forward cross-overs with the stick cradled atop the front of their shoulders. Coaches need to show them that this is intended to keep their shoulders balanced on the cross-over turns and not dipping inward. Over-coach here by telling them to keep the inside shoulder up.

Zone I stick
position:
(player facing)

Zone II stick
position:
(back of player)

Skaters in Zone II will work backward cross-under with the stick positioned behind their backs in the small of their back.

COACHING POINTS:
Shoulders parallel to the ice.

NAME OF DRILL: Timber! Stick Drill
SKILL TO BE TAUGHT/ENHANCED: Quick starts

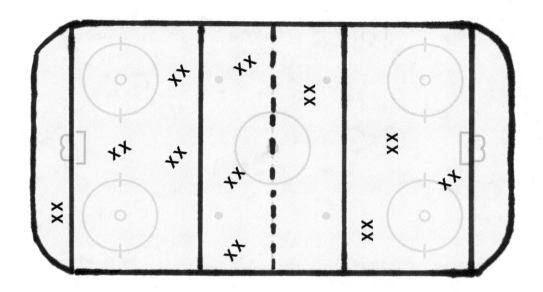

DESCRIPTION OF DRILL:
- Scatter your players in pairs all over the ice. Set them 4-8' apart based upon ability.
- Have them set their sticks upright on the butt-end just holding it erect until you blow the whistle. Each player then breaks for the other player's stick in attempt to grab it before it falls to the ice. A fun drill.

COACHING POINTS:
- Have the players employ good V-toe start position.
- Also, another way to execute this drill is to have each player race against his or her own stick. Stand it upright and then have them spin and catch the stick with the same hand.

NAME OF DRILL: Gloves-Off Figure-8s
SKILL TO BE TAUGHT/ENHANCED: Tight-turn in Skating

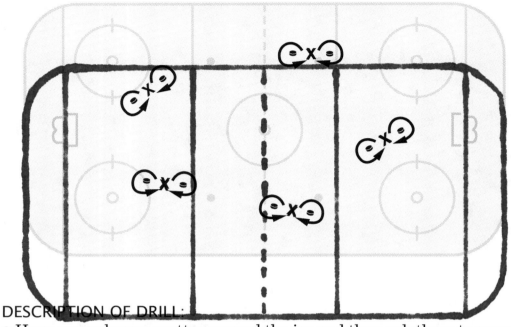

DESCRIPTION OF DRILL:

- Have your players scatter around the ice and then ask them to remove their hockey gloves. They should place them on the ice.
- On the whistle they must skate in figure 8 patterns around and between their gloves as shown above. Note that the gloves are between 6' and 10' apart depending upon the physical sizes of the players being drilled (tell them to place the glove roughly a body length apart).
- This drill can also be used as an excellent stickhandling drill if you add pucks. Have them work both forward and backward in their skating and add front and back skate pivots.

COACHING POINTS:
Emphasize crunching the back 1/3 of the skateblade into the ice. Also emphasize the inward lean creating a tight turning radius for the inside shoulder and further cite the importance of dropping down low at the knees. Skaters should also be told to place the inside leg of the turn in front of the outside leg, as shown.

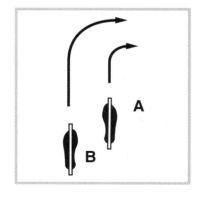

NAME OF DRILL: Ugly Ballerina Drills
SKILL TO BE TAUGHT/ENHANCED: Skating Agility, Balance
DURATION OF DRILL: 2-4 runs

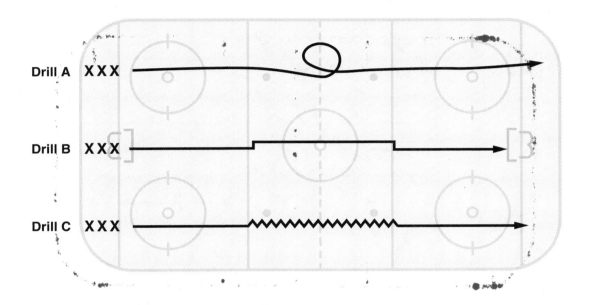

DESCRIPTION OF DRILL:
DRILL A:
Skater breaks for the red line, spins in a 360-degree full circle. Be sure to have players spin each way.
DRILL B:
Player skates through the neutral zone on one skate with chest over the glide leg (be sure to caution players against merely raising one skate off the ice by flexing knee — they must be fully balanced on one skate and have them spread their arms to the side as if they were flying).
DRILL C:
Skate to near blue line and run on the toes through the neutral zone. Emphasize quick feet and high knee action.

COACHING POINTS:
These drills are actually performed better en masse. Have all of your players line up behind the goalline and skate the length of the ice to work these drills rather than in individual series as above.

NAME OF DRILL: Drop Drills
SKILL TO BE TAUGHT/ENHANCED: Agility, Recovery in Skating

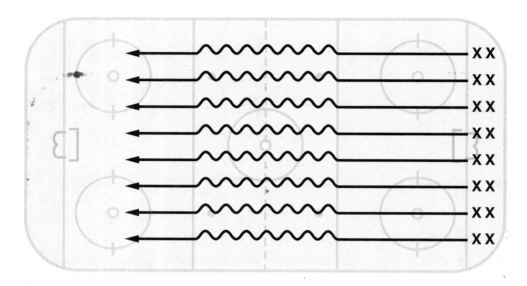

DESCRIPTION OF DRILL:
- This is a series of skating agility drills which call for the player to recover after having been fully or partially dropped to the ice.
- Line the players up at the endlines and have them skate the length of the ice through the neutral zone where most of the recovery work will be performed.

DRILL I: KNEE DROPS

Drop to one knee at the blue line (you can use either the left or right knee or alternate one different knee at each blue line).

DRILL II: DOUBLE KNEE DROPS

Drop to both knees at the red line and recover.

DRILL III: RICKEY HENDERSON DRILL

Dive full out at the red line landing on stomach, and recover. Why the name? Henderson slides into second base head-first doesn't he?

DRILL IV: DIVE–DROP–N–ROLL

Similar to the Henderson dive, emphasize the roll-over recovery employed in some situations.

DRILL V: RUSSIAN DANCER

Quickly alternate the knee drops all the way through the neutral zone. More advanced skaters can perform drills I, II, IV and V while skating backward.

NAME OF DRILL: Stop-n-Drop — Rise Again
SKILL TO BE TAUGHT/ENHANCED: Agility on the Ice

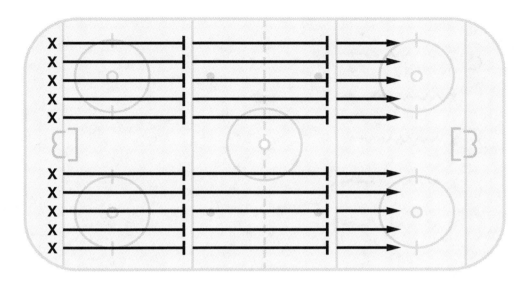

DESCRIPTION OF DRILL:
• This is a simple agility drill which can be of obvious use in a hockey game. Have the player skate the length of the ice, but stop, facing one sideboard, at each blue line.
• They will then drop to one knee, both knees or their stomachs.
• On your whistle, they must spring to their feet as quickly and efficiently as possible and break for the next line.

COACHING POINTS:
When the players are on their knees, have them hold their sticks straight out and with both hands on it as if they were cross-checking. This forces them to jump to their feet without the aid of a push with their hands on the ice.

NAME OF DRILL: Net Pushes and Net Pulls
SKILL TO BE TAUGHT/ENHANCED: Leg Strength, Backward Cross-under

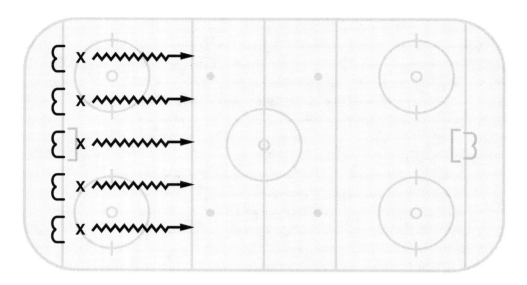

DESCRIPTION OF DRILL:
- Conventional hockey nets can be used in a variety of ways. Besides having teams of youth skaters push them the length of the ice in relay races (and this would include goalies) which have the hidden agenda of working to increase leg strength, nets can also be used as a teaching device.
- Place as many nets as you can rustle up along the goalline. Have the skaters face them and grip the crossbar (no sticks in hand, of course) After you have taught them the intricacies of the backward cross-under, with its weight shift and edge control inuendoes, have them pull the nets for the length of the ice employing this technique. You will find that they can more easily execute the backward cross-under in this fashion because the balance factor is neutralized much in the way that a developmental skater uses a chair to push himself along.

NAME OF DRILL: Iron Cross Drill
SKILL TO BE TAUGHT/ENHANCED: Agility
DURATION OF DRILL: 20-40 sec.

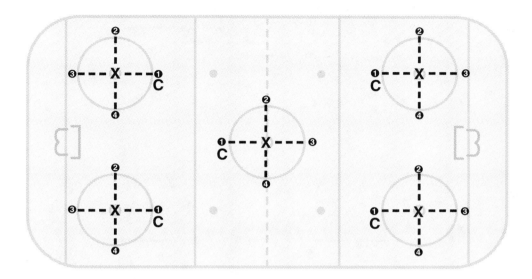

DESCRIPTION OF DRILL:
- Place a coach at each circle as shown and one player in the center of the circle at the dot.
- On the voice command of "One!" "Two!," "Three!" or "Four!," the player is to break as quickly as possible to the designed edge of the circle, points 1, 2, 3 or 4. The coach may use a stick or hand signals to direct the player.
- Be sure that the skaters use cross-over hop starts for lateral movement, sharp stops, "with the chips flying," and cross-under starts for the backskating.
- After reaching the edge of the circle, each player must quickly return to the center dot without hearing a command to do so. Obviously, the coach should vary the sequence of number commands.

COACHING POINTS:
- Use all five circles so that maximum ice surface is utilized; other players can be substituted for coaches. Spare players can be lined up along the boards or on the benches.
- Another variation of this drill is to add a stopwatch. Have the players, for example, execute this cross pattern four complete times in 30 seconds each way.

NAME OF DRILL: Wave Drill Crossovers
SKILL TO BE TAUGHT/ENHANCED: Skating Agility/Balance
DURATION OF DRILL: 2-4 sec.

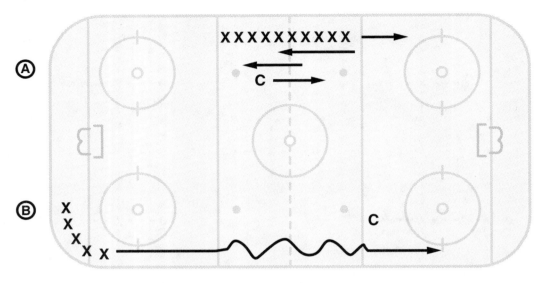

DESCRIPTION OF DRILL:
DRILL A:
- Align players facing the coach.
- As coach points direction with stick, players are to "dance" the cross-overs in that direction.
- Reverse the direction.
- Add in knee drops by pointing stick downward to one side. Players react by crossing over to that side and, when signalled, they drop to the one knee on that side, recovering quickly.

DRILL B:
Have the players break out from the corner and execute full-speed cross-overs upon the coach's command (i.e. point with stick). They must accelerate. Two to four cross-overs are all that is needed to impart the skill.

COACHING POINTS:
- This drill can be added in during laps to open the practice: as the players hit the neutral zone, they face the center ice circle, dancing the cross-over through the zone.
- Note that two types of cross-over maneuvers are being drilled here.

NAME OF DRILL: Zimmerman's "N" Drills
SKILL TO BE TAUGHT/ENHANCED: Skating, Puckhandling Skills

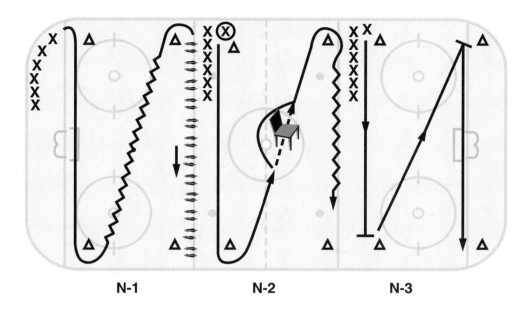

N-1   **N-2**   **N-3**

DESCRIPTION OF DRILL:
From a page taken out of coaching colleague Tim Zimmerman's drillbook, these drills can combine a variety of imaginative skills. Shown are three such skill-drills, always performed in the "N" configuration.
DRILL N-1:
Foreskate,backskate, side-carioca — break to the first cone, pivot into a backskate mode and then face up ice at the third cone "dancing" on the toes of the skates in a cross-over/cross-under side-hop.
DRILL N-2:
With a puck, foreskate to the first cone and execute a tight turn around it, deke the chair or cone placed at center ice and then when the third cone is reached, pivot into a backskating carry.
DRILL N-3:
Execute a sharp start-and-stop at each cone.

COACHING POINTS:
• Players can change into the next zone upon completing the drill in the preceeding zone or they can wait for the coach's call to change zones.
• Coaches can vary these drills as per need and imagination. Incorporate pivots, stops, tight turns, knee drops, etc., etc. with or without pucks.

NAME OF DRILL: Z-Drills: Series I
SKILL TO BE TAUGHT/ENHANCED: Skating, Stops and Starts

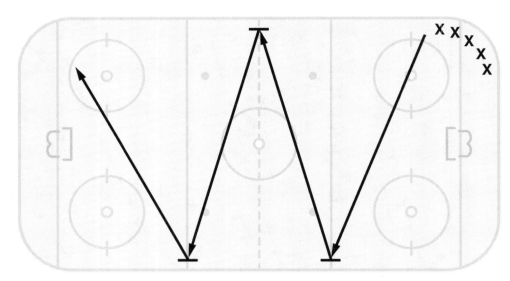

◀——— **Face this way for this series of stops**

DESCRIPTION OF DRILL:
- Align players in corners as shown and, on whistle, they must break for blue line and red line corners performing designated stops.
- Make sure that the players all face the designated and singular direction when they stop so that they will work on stopping to both sides.
- Rather than simply performing "stops," enhance the skill by calling upon the players to execute these maneuvers:
     — One-legged stops with right or left skate (lead skate)
     — Stop and then cross-over to accelerate
     — Stop, pivot to backskate and backskate to next stopping area
     — Stop, spin out and go

COACHING POINTS:
Players will cheat on this drill by not coming to a full stop or by stopping only the side they are proficient in. Be wary.

NAME OF DRILL: Z-Drills: Series II
SKILL TO BE TAUGHT/ENHANCED: Skating Agility

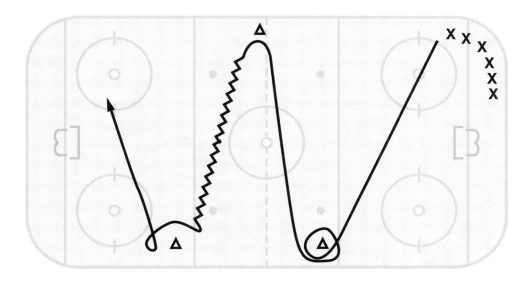

DESCRIPTION OF DRILL:
- Align the players for this series just as you did for series I except that cones will demarcate the skill-performance area in this series.
- With the players coming out of the corners, have them perform such maneuvers as:
    — Tight turns (a.k.a: "hockey turns")*
    — Mohawk turns (toes are turned out on both skates)
    — 360-degree spins
    — Pivots to backskate
    — Stop, cross-over agility to next cones, etc.

COACHING POINTS:
In this entire series (I and II), it is advisable to station a coach at each drill area.

*In executing the tight turn, or hockey turn, I am at odds with many conventional powerskating instructors in that I allow my skaters to dip the inside shoulder into the turn (other instructors tell the skaters to keep the shoulders parallel to the ice). My reasons are twofold: a) dipping the inside shoulders will tighten the turning radius as a matter of physics; b) look at films and photos — everyone doing this turn does in fact dip their shoulders!

NAME OF DRILL: Z-Drills: III
SKILL TO BE TAUGHT/ENHANCED: Stops, Starts, Acceleration

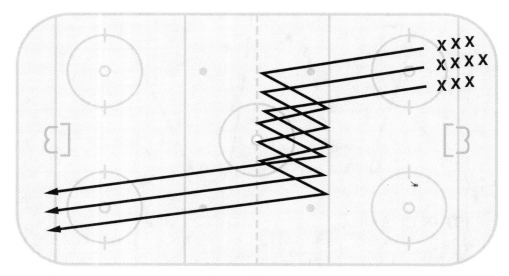

Face this way

DESCRIPTION OF DRILL:
- Form three lines, as shown.
- On whistle, the three lines will break into the neutral zone simultaneously and perform alternate side stops. Be sure that the players face the sideboards as indicated.

COACHING POINTS:
- To maximize ice surface, this drill can be performed with another set of three lines beginning at the opposite faceoff circle mirroring the drill in their half of the neutral zone.
- This drill can also be done for the full length of the ice surface by setting two lines of cones through the faceoff dots.

NAME OF DRILL: Z-Drills: IV
SKILL TO BE TAUGHT/ENHANCED: Forskate/Backskate Transition
Agility

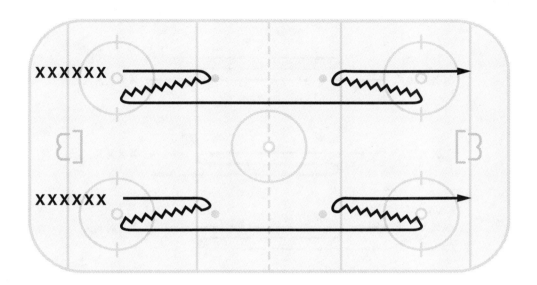

DESCRIPTION OF DRILL:
- Form two lines and have players break to neutral zone dot; they quickly jam into a backskate mode to the faceoff dot and then...
- Return up ice to far endzone dot, jam into backskate mode again as they return to the far neutral zone dot and then...
- Break up ice to far endline.
- If the dots are too faint to read on the ice, coaches can perform this drill using the lines: forward to the far blue line, backskate to the near blue line and then pivot and break up ice to the far goalline.

COACHING POINTS:
- Coaches must emphasize speed and quickness in this drill.
- Also, be sure that the players perform all of their pivots to the same side, replicating the drill with opposite side pivots when they return up ice.
- Advanced players can execute this drill with pucks.

NAME OF DRILL: Z-Drills: V
SKILL TO BE TAUGHT/ENHANCED: Skating, Tight Turns

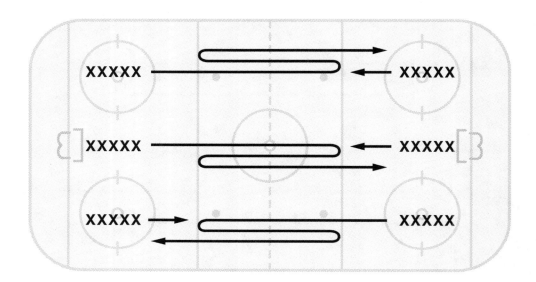

DESCRIPTION OF DRILL:
- Work this drill from both ends of the rink at the same time.
- Align the players in three lines at each end as shown.
- On the whistle the lead players break for the far blue line, execute a tight turn toward the boards, return to the near blue line and execute another tight turn, again facing the boards. They then break for the other end of the ice.
- Emphasize speed and keeping the head up since collisions can occur. And always turn toward the boards!
- As for which way the middle line turns, simply designate a preferred side by telling them to turn toward the bench, the scoreboard or whatever.

NAME OF DRILL: Z-Drills: VI
SKILL TO BE TAUGHT/ENHANCED: Skating Agility, Fore/Backskate;
Pivots, Stops

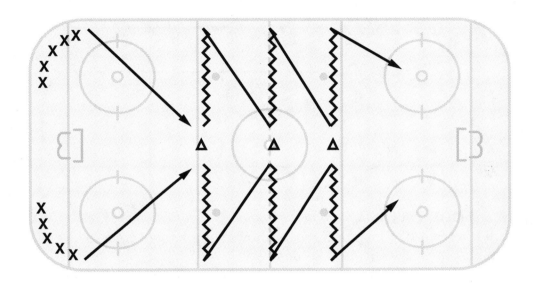

DESCRIPTION OF DRILL:
- Align the players in the corners and three cones in the neutral zone as shown.
- On the whistle, the lead players in each line will break, in a foreskate mode to the first cone, pivot into the backskating mode along the appropriate line, pivot back into a foreskate and repeat to and from the next two cones.

NAME OF DRILL: Pretzel Drill
SKILL TO BE TAUGHT/ENHANCED: Skating

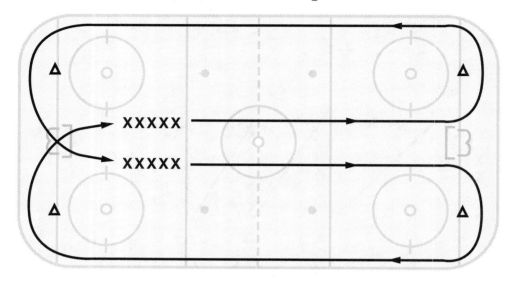

DESCRIPTION OF DRILL:
- Skate pretzel-like loop pattern as shown; emphasize cross-overs, speed.
- Can add in backskating if so desired.
- Can add whistle pattern whereby skaters change from foreskate to backskate on whistle — the more whistles, the more changes and hence, more agility.
- Think about adding pucks to this drill so that players can work on control and pivots.
- Make this drill and "overspeed" drill by emphasizing acceleration and having the players "keep their feet moving."

NAME OF DRILL: 5-Circle Drill: With/Without Pucks

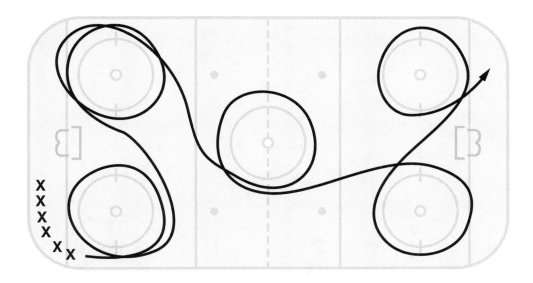

DESCRIPTION OF DRILL:
WITHOUT PUCKS:
Emphasize the cross-over when foreskating and the crossunder when backskating through this drill. Emphasize the thrust of the toe into the ice with the trailing skate. More advanced skaters can make this into a valuable agility drill by emphasizing "running on the toes."
WITH PUCKS:
Employ this drill both foreskating and backskating with the pucks. Coaches also can call for their players to skate the circles using one hand to control the puck. Another skill-enhancement sequence is to emphasize the puck being carried to the outside of the circle with the puck carrier's body between the puck and an imaginary checker (lean inward in utilizing this latter skill).

COACHING POINTS:
Returning to the argument earlier about whether or not to dip the inside shoulder into the turn, I suggested that it is acceptable to do this on the "tight turn" or "hockey turn." In cross-over turns it is more beneficial, in terms of balance, to keep the inside shoulder up. While there will be a natural tendency to dip the inside shoulder, have your players strive to keep their shoulder at least parallel to the ice on cross-over turns.

NAME OF DRILL: Pivot Drill
SKILL TO BE TAUGHT/ENHANCED: Skating

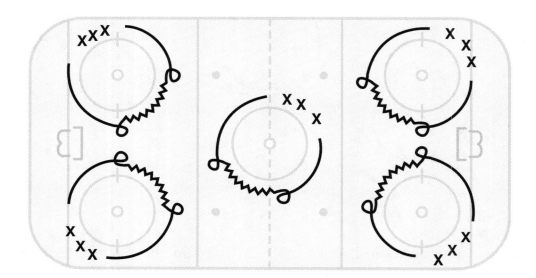

DESCRIPTION OF DRILL:
- Can use all 5 circles for this drill.
- As players skate the circles, they must pivot to backskate/foreskate on whistle.
- Emphasize acceleration, not just the pivot.
- Rather than 5 groups, various patterns can be employed:
  - 3 circles diagonally up the ice
  - 2 endzone circles in figure-8 patterns

COACHING POINTS:
Bring the heels together to form a "V" when executing the pivot.

NAME OF DRILL: Five-Circle Variation
SKILL TO BE TAUGHT/ENHANCED: Skating, Agility, Pivots

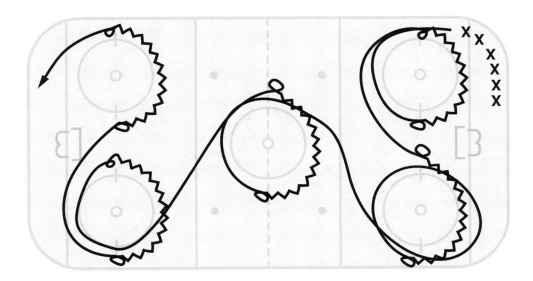

DESCRIPTION OF DRILL:
- Line the players in one corner as shown and proceed to work the conventional five-circle cross-over skating drill.
- The difference here is that the players must constantly face up ice so that they will have to foreskate and then backskate, always crossing over and crossing under as the technique warrants.

NAME OF DRILL: Full-Ice 3-Circle Drill
SKILL TO BE TAUGHT/ENHANCED: Foreskate/Backskate Turns Speed

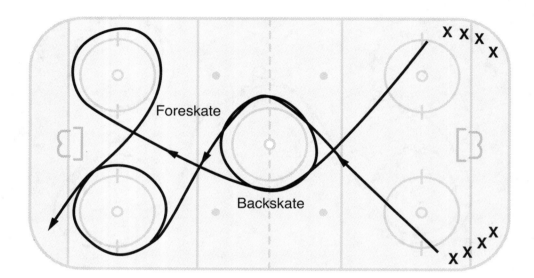

DESCRIPTION OF DRILL:
- Two lines go simultaneously; speed is emphasized.
- Can use full ice and return to 5-circle drill, but endurance becomes factor then.
- Combine backskating and foreskating by designating different circles for each skill; you may wish to keep entire drill foreskating and then switch to backskating to emphasize/reinforce.
- Once proficiency is gained, use pucks.

NAME OF DRILL: 4-Dot Drill
SKILL TO BE TAUGHT/ENHANCED: Quickness, Tight Turns

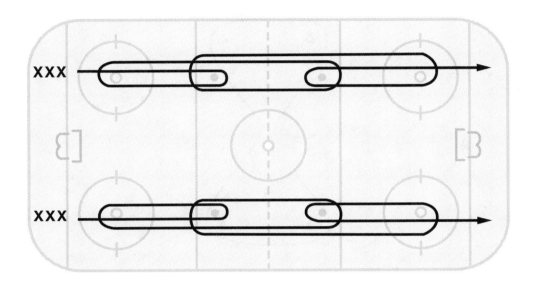

DESCRIPTION OF DRILL:
- Skate 2 lines simultaneously.
- Note the numbering of the dots; pylons may be used.
- Player skates to dot #2, turns to his right and skates back to dot 1, again turning to his right to break up ice, skating to dot 3 whereupon he turns right again, skating back to dot 2. Turning to his right again, he breaks for dot 4, turns right, tightly, and swiftly, skating back to dot 3. After rounding dot 3, again with a right-hand turn, he breaks for endboards.
- Repeat sequence (2-1-3-2-4-3) with left-hand tight turns.
- Always turn to the inside of the rink and when both halves of the surface are used, players will execute turns both ways.

NAME OF DRILL: Peanut Drills
SKILL TO BE TAUGHT/ENHANCED: Skating, Turns, Acceleration

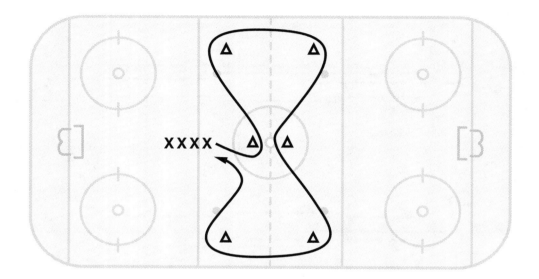

DESCRIPTION OF DRILL:
- With smaller players, all three zones can be utilized by setting up a "peanut" in each.
- Have the players follow the course as shown, but they are to work on designated skills such as tight turns, pivots, cross-overs out of the turn, etc. They can employ Mohawk turns (both toes pointed out) as well as backskating around the peanut performing cross-unders. Ask your players to make their turns on one skate to emphasize the "bite" of the edge into the ice.

COACHING POINTS:
- Peanut drills can also be used with pucks.
- Use imagination here. Many drills can emanate from this set-up.

NAME OF DRILL: "88s"
SKILL TO BE TAUGHT/ENHANCED: Skating Cross-overs, Acceleration

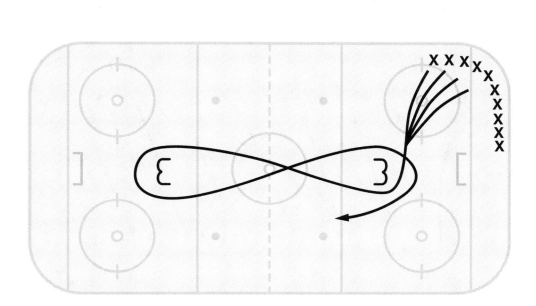

DESCRIPTION OF DRILL:
• Place nets at top of each deep faceoff circle, as shown.
• Send players out in sets of four to six to skate figure-8's around the nets, accelerating into cross-over turns, running on their toes and trying to catch the leader. They should each skate two to four laps around the course.

NAME OF DRILL: 8-Dot Tite-Turn Drill
SKILL TO BE TAUGHT/ENHANCED: Skating and Turns

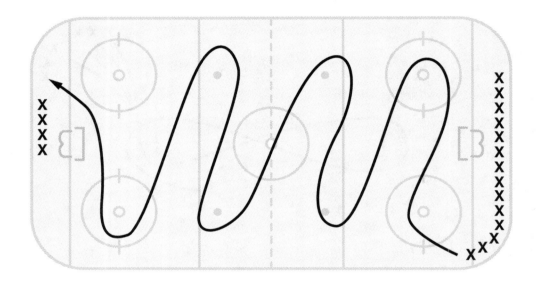

DESCRIPTION OF DRILL:
- Line the players in the corner and endboards, as shown.
- On the whistle they will burst from the corner, one-by-one, and execute a series of tight turns around the faceoff dots, all eight of them.
- Some coaches like to have their players use the "hand-down" technique whereby they have the player place their inside arm and hand down to the ice to enhance the center of gravity (i.e., getting low to the ice).
- It is also a good idea to have the players, when coming out of the turn, execute a cross-over step to re-accelerate.

COACHING POINTS:
Note how the angle of the dots forces a tighter turn. I have seen coaches use cones in a tight, half-ice sequence, too.

NAME OF DRILL: Box Drill
SKILL TO BE TAUGHT/ENHANCED: Skating, High Speed Maneuvering

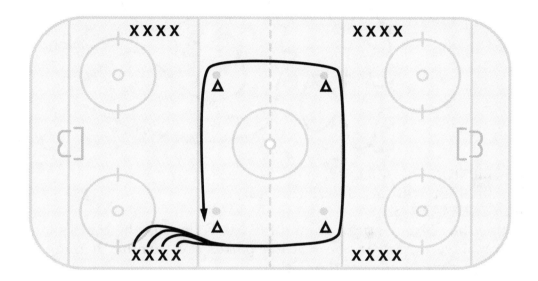

DESCRIPTION OF DRILL:
- Similar to the small-zone combination drills described elsewhere, this sequence employs higher speeds, greater agility and more endurance.
- Align the players in four groups as shown. Players will burst from the lines designated by the coach on the whistle. They will skate as a group of four to six skaters.
- Skating maneuvers to be employed:
  — Cross-over accelerations around cones
  — Cross-under accelerations around cones
  — Foreskate to one cone, pivot to backskate to next cone,etc.
  — Foreskate to first cone, carioca cross-over to next cone, etc.

NAME OF DRILL: Follow The Leader/Obstacle Course
SKILL TO BE TAUGHT/ENHANCED: Skating Agility, Overall Skills

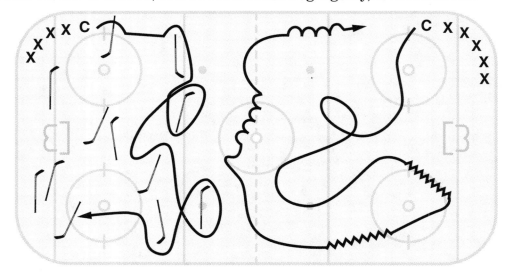

DESCRIPTION OF DRILL:
Two different drills are described here.
OBSTACLE COURSE:
Scatter the players' sticks around the ice. Following the coach's lead, a line of players repeats the skating pattern of turning, leaping, etc., through, around and over the sticks.
FOLLOW THE LEADER:
This is similar to the drill described above. The difference is that there are no stick-obstacles on the ice. This allows the lead-coach to perform spins, backskating, running on the toes and so forth.

COACHING POINTS:
• Look at your skaters. See what they need work in. If it is stopping, then add this into your lead-pattern in either drill. If it is backskating or tight turns, then emphasize those. Be observant.
• Another way to fashion the obstacle course is to lay the sticks, in railroad track fashion, along the sideboards as shown here:

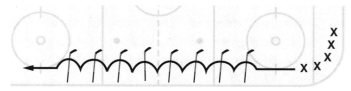

Skaters will emphasize quick feet.

NAME OF DRILL: Multi-Skill Drill
SKILL TO BE TAUGHT/ENHANCED: Skating Agility

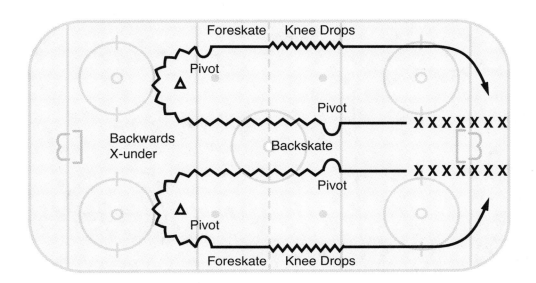

DESCRIPTION OF DRILL:
- Line the players up in two lines around and off the goalpost.
- On the whistle, the two lead players break for the neutral zone and pivot into a backskate — they must pivot toward each other.
- They then backskate, crossing under to accelerate around the cones as shown and then pivot into a foreskate mode, again turning toward each other to return to the neutral zone.
- Have them execute a series of alternating knee drops (i.e., drop one knee to the ice and then recover to drop the other knee) between the red line and the blue line as shown.
- Return and switch lines.

COACHING POINTS:
No pucks.

NAME OF DRILL: Combo Drills
SKILL TO BE TAUGHT/ENHANCED: Skating, Agility

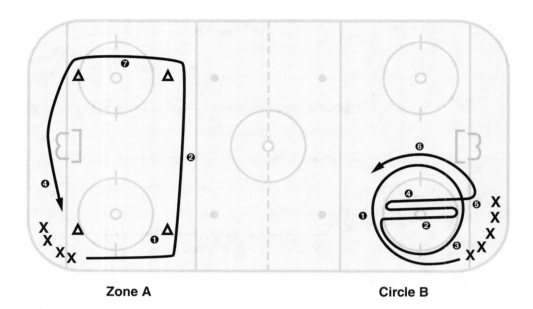

Zone A   **Circle B**

DESCRIPTION OF DRILL:
Use imagination here. The seven basic skills to impart are:
1. Foreskate and stop
2. Backskate and pivot to foreskate
3. Foreskate and pivot to backskate
4. Backskate and stop
5. Cross-overs (foreskating)
6. Cross-unders (backskating)
7. Side-straddle cross-overs (carioca of a sorts)
Using either circles or zone with pylons squaring the area off, set up a schemata in which players use each of the skills. A typical sequence may be that described in Zone A or that noted in circle B.

NAME OF DRILL: Rats In The Maze Drill
SKILL TO BE TAUGHT/ENHANCED: Skating, Agility, Quickness

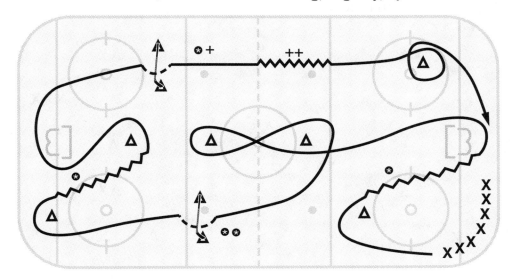

DESCRIPTION OF DRILL:
- The "course" need not be laid out exactly as shown; creativity can be encouraged here.
- Begin the players in the corners and send them through the course in pairs or threes. Note the annotations:
    *backskate
    **leap
    *+ dive-and-recover
    ++ side-hops/carioca drill

COACHING POINTS:
- Place a coach at as many areas/stations as possible since directions will be needed and re-setting of obstacles which get knocked over will be necessary.
- An interesting addition to the maze is to place the nets facing each other about 2-to-3 feet apart and slightly ajar. Have the skaters weave through them! Younger skaters love it; call it "The Cave!"

NAME OF DRILL: Three Cones/Three Drills
SKILL TO BE TAUGHT/ENHANCED: Skating Agility
DURATION OF DRILL: 30 sec.

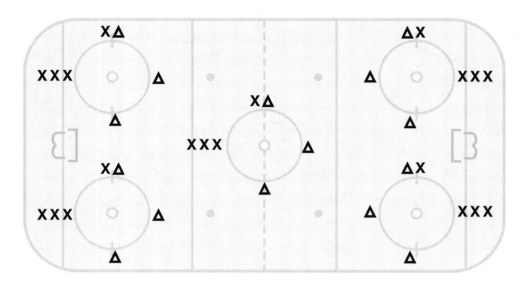

DESCRIPTION OF DRILL:
- Set three cones, triangulated, on the perimeter of each faceoff circle. Then divide your team into five groups for the purposes of this skating agility and quick-feet drill.
- To begin the drill, have one player step up and position himself at one of the lower cones. On the whistle, they will execute any of several skating pattern you call for:

> A) Foreskate to cone 3, pivot and backskate to cone 1; repeat.
> B) Backskate to cone 3, pivot and foreskate to cone 1; repeat.
> C) Foreskate all three cones, tight-turning each as if you were executing a circle escape.

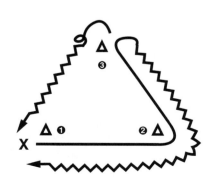

NAME OF DRILL: Four Corners/Four Drills
SKILL TO BE TAUGHT/ENHANCED: Skating Agility

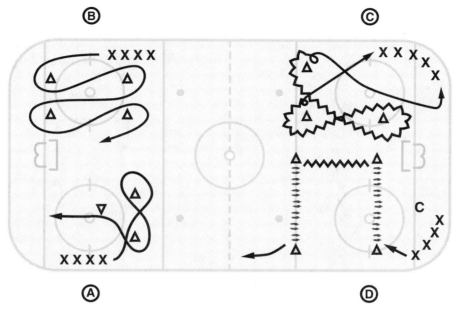

DESCRIPTION OF DRILL:
DRILL A:
On whistle, skater figure-8's through the cones and then leaps the two cones lying on their side end-to-end.
DRILL B:
Forward tight turns around and through the cones as shown.
DRILL C:
Backward turns and acceleration through and around the cones as shown.
DRILL D:
On whistle, player breaks for near cone, pivots quickly to face the coach, executes cross-over carioca steps from cone-to-cone, backskates to the far set of cones and repeats the crossovers the other way, always facing the coach.

COACHING POINTS:
- Drills B and C can be done with pucks, but only if the skaters are advanced since pucks will slow the drills down and have the effect of altering the concentration of the players.
- Depending upon the total number of players you are working with, these stations may only run for as little as two minutes each. Keep the tempo high.

NAME OF DRILL: Stepper
SKILL TO BE TAUGHT/ENHANCED: Skating, Knee Flexion, Agility, Stride

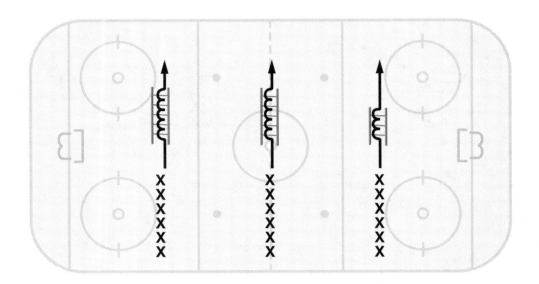

DESCRIPTION OF DRILL:
- The Stepper resembles as large ladder. It is made of 2' x 4' wood, 6' in length, with 1" dowels spaced 18" apart. The Stepper is 2' wide.
- Have players line up and "run-start" through the Stepper. Emphasize their knee flexion, toe push, short-stride acceleration and "V" in their skate alignment.
- In a sense, this drill replicates the old "run the tires" drill done by football coaches since time immemorial.

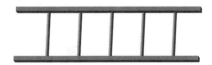

COACHING POINTS:
- Make the Stepper out of wood since this will not chip or dull skate blades when it gets stepped on, which it inevitably will.
- In teaching this drill, be sure to have the skaters begin the acceleration on their toes. It can be beneficial to have them touch their heels together also.

NAME OF DRILL: Stick-Rope Drills
SKILL TO BE TAUGHT/ENHANCED: Skating, Balance, Agility, Weight Transfer

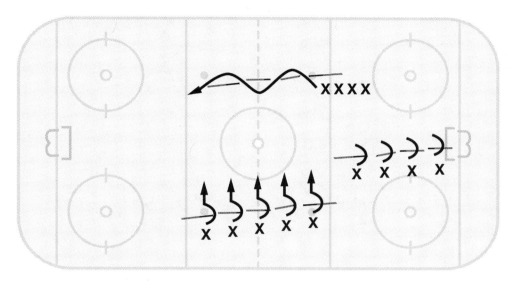

DESCRIPTION OF DRILL:
- First of all, a "stick rope" must be constructed from broken hockey sticks cut into 3' lengths and joined, hinge-fashion, with small metal single-holed braces and 1 1/2" screws with bolts. Piece four such sticks together and you will have a 12' length of "stick rope" which is easily stored, carried and used on the ice.
- Drills: 2-foot hops over the stick, cross-over strides both forward and backward, 2-foot side-straddle hops, cross-over starts, etc.

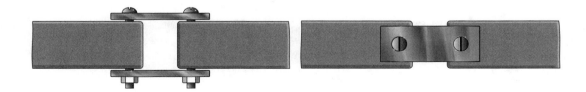

NAME OF DRILL: Leap, Spin, Dive

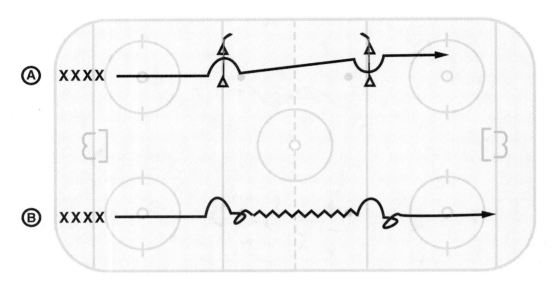

DESCRIPTION OF DRILL:
DRILL A:
Lay a stick across two cones (you may have to lay the cone on its side for the leaping portion of this drill so that the height is not prohibitive). Players will leap over one set of cone/stick hurdles, and they will dive under the other set.
DRILL B:
Have the players fully leap, with both skates leaving the ice, as they turn into their backskate and return into their foreskate. This is for agility purposes only; they will not use such a leap in game conditions!
ANCILLARY TO THIS DRILL:
Have the players perform turns from foreskate to backskate on one skate. Be sure to repeat with the other skate (no leaping here!) and in either case described, be sure to work their turns to both sides.

COACHING POINTS:
I have also seen a drill similar to this one in which sideline benches are used and players must dive under and/or leap over the benches.

NAME OF DRILL: Mohawk Turns Drill
SKILL TO BE TAUGHT/ENHANCED: "Mohawk" Turn

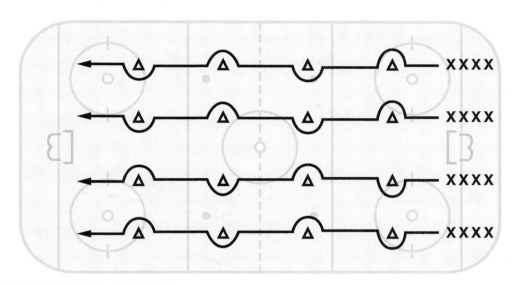

DESCRIPTION OF DRILL:
- In this sequential drill, have the players simply stand in a duckfooted position with their toes out. Have them place their heels about shoulder-width apart. (some coaches talk of a heels-together position; I prefer a shoulder-width and photos of players executing this turn verify my belief.)
- Have them lean over a glove so that their chest is in a position over the glove. Then have them push off one toe and feel the spin. Be careful in that you can get dizzy demonstrating this!
- Next form lines and set cones up the ice so that the turn can be worked to both sides.

COACHING POINTS:
- You may prefer to have the players actually walk in their "duckwalk" stances to help learn the footwork.
- Also, strive to keep the knees at a 90-degree angle.
- Futhermore, have the players execute these turns in a slow, controlled fashion to learn the skill.

NAME OF DRILL: Run The Gauntlet (II)
SKILL TO BE TAUGHT/ENHANCED: Skating Agility, Balance

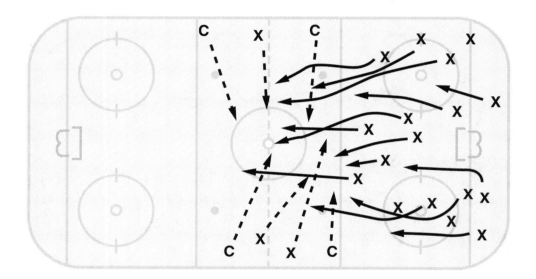

DESCRIPTION OF DRILL:
- Line players up in one end of ice and have coaches set up along boards in neutral zone.
- Coaches are to be "armed" with tennis balls or pucks.
- As players skate through the neutral zone, coaches hit them with thrown tennis balls or pucks shot at their skates.
- If hit, players must join coaches.
- Repeat with players skating from other direction.

NAME OF DRILL: Glantz's Four Dot Circle Drill
SKILL TO BE TAUGHT/ENHANCED: Cross-overs, Cross-unders

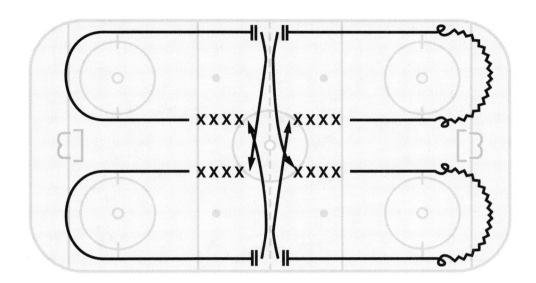

DESCRIPTION OF DRILL:
• Set four lines of skaters in the neutral zone as shown.
• On the whistle they are to break for the circles and accelerate with good hard cross-overs emphasizing the push off both skates (we often forget about pushing with the outside edge of the "under" skate — see the Providence College drill outlined earlier).
• Emphasize acceleration.
• Work backward cross-unders, too, and emphasize the "pull" of inside skate.
• Conclude with a good, crisp stop at the red line and then have the player line up on the opposite line so that he/she can work the skating turn to the opposite direction.

STICKHANDLING DRILLS

"Long meetings are B.S. The mind can only absorb what the rear end can endure."

Coach Terry Crisp

NAME OF DRILL: Stationary Stickhandling Drills
SKILL TO BE TAUGHT/ENHANCED: Stickhandling, "Attacking the Triangle"

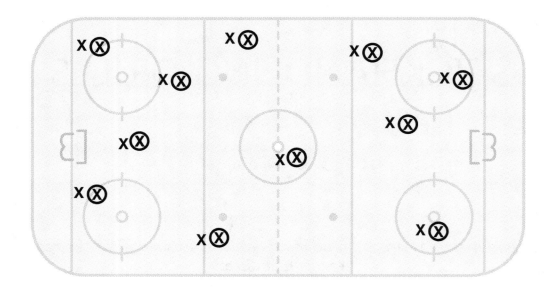

DESCRIPTION OF DRILL:
DRILL A: (see drawing on next page)
- Align partners of players in scattered positions around the rink.
- One of the two partners will stand still with their stick at arms length in front of them, tripod fashion.
- "Attacker" with the puck will dribble the puck side-to-side but through the dummy defender's triangle (i.e. underneath his stick and in front of the legs).
Do this with two hands and then with one hand and work both the top hand and the bottom hand.
- Now allow movement from the attacker. He/she must slip the puck through the legs, through the stick and legs, etc. skating quickly and pivoting around the still stationary dummy defender.*

stickhandling   dummy
attacker   defender

DRILL B: (not diagrammed)
Have players perform individual and stationary stickhandling on their knees. This teaches them to keep their hands away from their bodies and it further enhances stick-tip (toe) control.

COACHING POINTS:
*Amplifying Drill A, have the players skate slowly down the ice, one-on-one and facing each other as attacker and tripod. Simply have the tripod player skate slowly backward as the "attacker" dingledangles the puck in and about.

NAME OF DRILL: Lap Drills with Pucks
SKILL TO BE TAUGHT/ENHANCED: Puck Control
DURATION OF DRILL: 5 min.

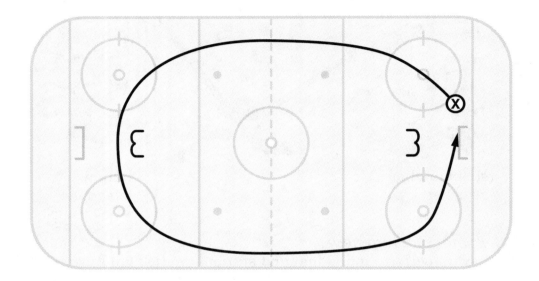

DESCRIPTION OF DRILL:
- As a drill unto itself or as part of your pre-practice routine, this drill enhances puck control by replicating most of all of your warm-up drills that you do without pucks.
- Do the same drills but add pucks — foreskate/backskate pivots, knee drops, stop-n-go, tight turns, leaps and spins, running, cross-overs, backward cross-unders, dives, etc.
- Note that the nets are positioned on the hashmarks.

COACHING POINTS:
- Make sure that the players' sticks are the correct length. Cut them off at the "Adam's Apple" as they hold the stick upright in front of them with their skates on. (Yes, this does differ from some conventional notions, but a shortened stick will enhance puck control at all levels of play!)
- Concerning the distance of the hands-relationship on the stick, one hand is on the knob, of course, but the other can be anywhere between a glove-length away or a forearm away for stickhandling purposes.

NAME OF DRILL: 1-on-1 Stationary Keep-Away
SKILL TO BE TAUGHT/ENHANCED: Stickhandling, Use of Body as a Shield
DURATION OF DRILL: 10-20 sec.

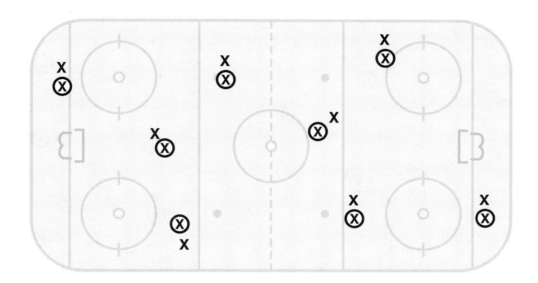

DESCRIPTION OF DRILL:
• Arrange players in pairs of roughly equal size and skill.
• They are to remain in one spot rather than skate around.
• One player is given the puck and the other must take it away using the poke check, stick-lift or "muscling" the body off the puck. The player with the puck must keep his hands dribbling the puck and his body between the puck and the checker.

COACHING POINTS:
A good way to learn the basic body positioning is to first perform the drill without sticks. Just have one player shift his/her body to keep it between the puck and the checker.

NAME OF DRILL: Close-Quarters One-On-One
SKILL TO BE TAUGHT/ENHANCED: Stickhandling, Quick Hands

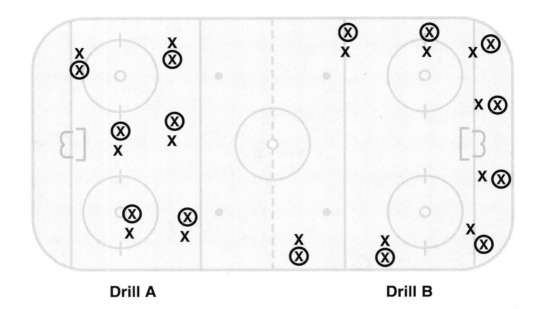

Drill A   **Drill B**

DESCRIPTION OF DRILL:
DRILL A:
Pair up your players and set them one stick-length apart. On the whistle
they are to retain the puck with quick stickhandling moves, feints and
dekes while the other player defends. They are scattered all over the
open ice, facing each other.
DRILL B:
- Perform the same drill with both players facing the boards. Now one
  player must escape and/or retain the puck. This simulates the essence
  of "mucking," so crucial to winning hockey.
- In drill A, the players must remain facing each other and in one gen-
  eral spot; in drill B the key is for the puck carrier to position his "butt
  to the pressure." The non-puck carrying checker may use his/her body
  to pin the carrier along the boards and the carrier should use his/her
  skates to keep control of the puck.
- Note that this drill is slightly different from the stationary 1-1 described elsewhere since in that drill one player is set behind the puck-
  carrier and the skill to be taught is body positioning. That is important
  here, too, but lesser so.

NAME OF DRILL: Heads Up Drill
SKILL TO BE TAUGHT/ENHANCED: Stickhandling, Keeping the Head Up

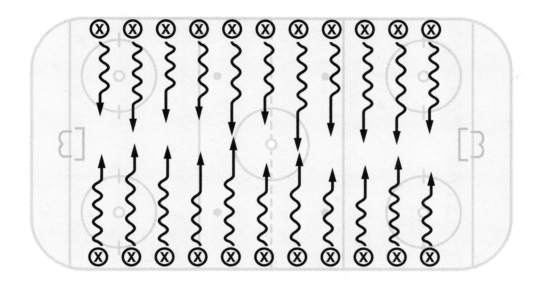

DESCRIPTION OF DRILL:
- Players will line up on opposite sides of the rink as shown.
- On the whistle they will stickhandle/carry the puck directly across the ice, emphasizing the point that they must keep their heads up. Failure to do so will mean a collision.
- Repeat the drill from the other direction.

NAME OF DRILL: Five-Circle Stickhandling
SKILL TO BE TAUGHT/ENHANCED: Stickhandling, Puck Control
DURATION OF DRILL: 60-90 sec.

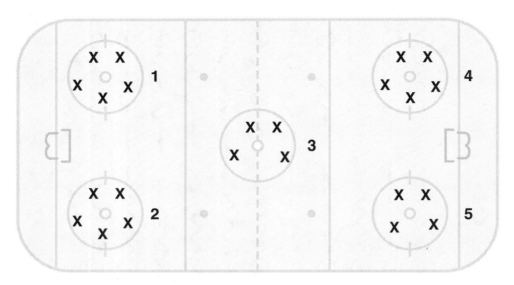

DESCRIPTION OF DRILL:
This sequence of 90-second drills incorporates virtually all aspects of
stickhandling.
CIRCLE #1:
Two-handed carrying within the circle — keep your head up since the
circle is crowded.
CIRCLE #2:
One-handed carry with only the top hand being used.
CIRCLE #3:
One-handed carry with only the bottom hand being use
CIRCLE #4:
No sticks — control and carry with skates only.
CIRCLE #5:
Airborne pucks — "dribble" in the air with the puck being bounced up-
ward off the stickface.
Set this drill in the following way — establish a route through all five
circles and blow a whistle every 90 seconds — then 30 seconds to ro-
tate, 90, 30, 90, etc.

COACHING POINTS:
Note that all players are working simultaneously here.

NAME OF DRILL: Three Zones Of Cones Drill
SKILL TO BE TAUGHT/ENHANCED: Stickhandling, Shooting

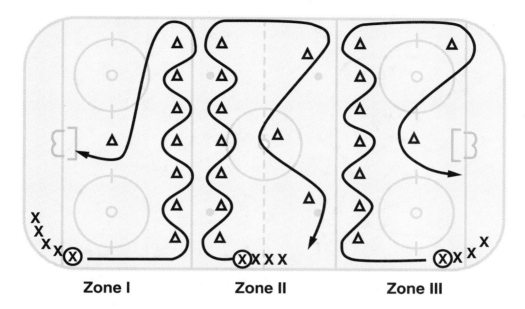

Zone I   **Zone II**   **Zone III**

DESCRIPTION OF DRILL:
- These drills are fairly standard and self-explanatory.
- Divide the team into three groups and have them work their way through the cone-courses as shown. You may wish to emphasize a different shot technique in each zone.
- Another more advanced variation may be to emphasize, e.g., top hand control in one zone, bottom hand in another and then both hands, or even skates, in the third zone.

COACHING POINTS:
Coaches, if you are light on cones and find yourself in need of things to demarcate "cones," drop your gloves, whistle and hat on the ice! (Yes, I put the fear of the Almighty into the kid who skates across my hat!)

NAME OF DRILL: More Cone Drills
SKILL TO BE TAUGHT/ENHANCED: Stickhandling, Puck Control

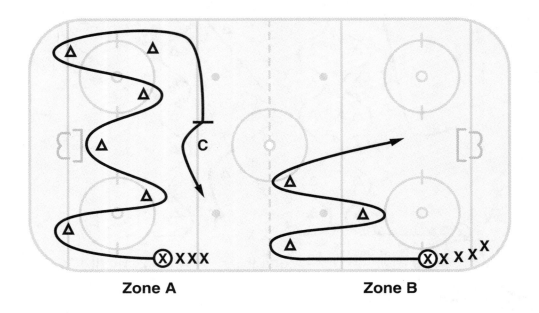

Zone A   **Zone B**

DESCRIPTION OF DRILL:
As coaches we can never get enough cone drills! Here are two more.
Zone A's drill involves tight turns and dekes while Zone B's drill calls for
    higher speed tight turns to be finished off with a shot.

NAME OF DRILL: Cone Clusters
SKILL TO BE TAUGHT/ENHANCED: Stickhandling Turns, Escapes

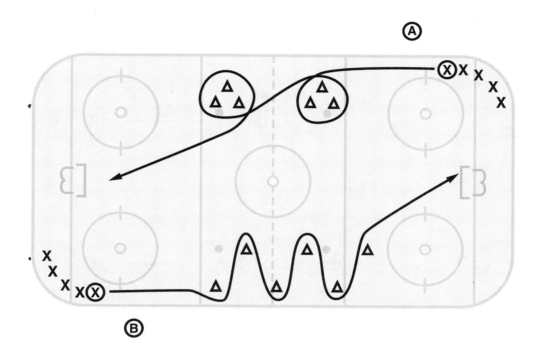

DESCRIPTION OF DRILL:
- There are two drills run simultaneously here.
- Group A performs tight-turn escapes around the cluster of 3 cones placed at each blue line. They must skate their tight turn with a puck and do so in the opposite direction at each cone cluster. They can then break for the net to make a shot on goal.
- Group B simply works their way through the cones spaced at wide diagonals.
- Switch lines when through.

COACHING POINTS:
- Cupping the stick is to be emphasized.
- Players skating the wide-diagonal cones in Group B should employ a cross-over at each turn.
- This drill, as conceived here, is for more advanced players and should be done at high-tempo. If players are less skilled, use only one cone for Group A and a more linear arrangement to the cone placement for Group B.

NAME OF DRILL: Quick Hands Drill
SKILL TO BE TAUGHT/ENHANCED: Puck Control

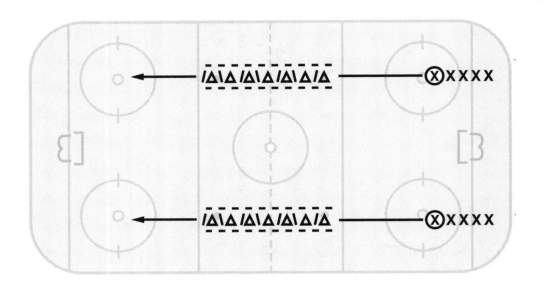

DESCRIPTION OF DRILL:
- Use smaller traffic cones for this drill if they are available. Have them lined up 4' apart in linear formation in the neutral zone and set up lines of players, with pucks, to work against the cones.
- As the player attacks the cones they are to <u>straddle</u> them and work the puck in and out. This creates a different dimension to the traditional "cone drill." It also helps quicken the stickhandlers' hands.
- You may elect to finish the drill with a shot on goal.

NAME OF DRILL: 3-Zone Stickhandling Turns
SKILL TO BE TAUGHT/ENHANCED: Stickhandling

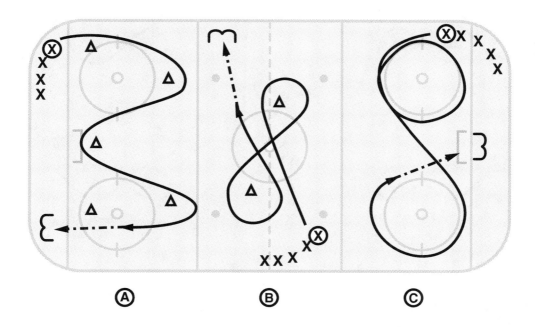

DESCRIPTION OF DRILL:
Fairly self-explanatory as diagrammed, these three drills are designed
to enhance stickhandling skills and can be performed at speeds relative
to the ages of the players involved.
ZONE A:
A huge S-shaped route through the cones culminating with a shot on
goal.
ZONE B:
A figure-8 pattern through the cones culminating in a shot on goal.
ZONE C:
Players should skate the circles and conclude with a shot on goal.

NAME OF DRILL: Figure-8's With Pucks
SKILL TO BE TAUGHT/ENHANCED: Stickhandling

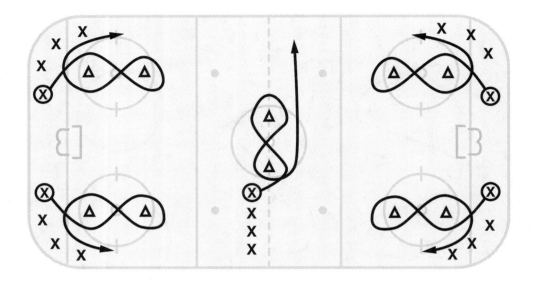

DESCRIPTION OF DRILL:
- Set players in as many as five groups.
- Place a cone at each opposite edge of a circle.
- On whistle, players are to carry through and around cones in figure-8 patterns.
- For players in the endzone circles, have them turn toward the boards first.

COACHING POINTS:
This technique comes off the figure-8 "tight turn" skating drill described elsewhere, so coaches may have to remind players of the appropriate skating skills.

NAME OF DRILL: 3-In-1 Stickhandling Drill
SKILL TO BE TAUGHT/ENHANCED: Stickhandling, 1-on-1 Moves

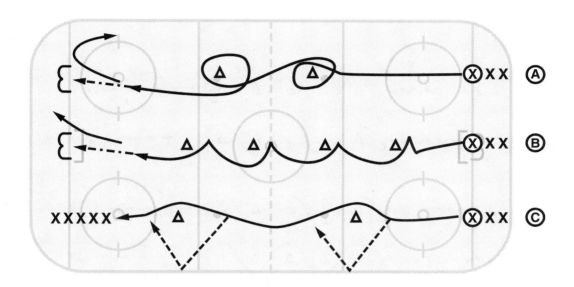

DESCRIPTION OF DRILL:
LINE A:

Performs tight hockey turn around pylon, dipping inside arm down to shield/ward off defender. More advanced players can work on full "spina-rama" circle move. Take a shot on goal.

LINE B   :

Dekes each cone by faking right and drawing left — they will make this same deke at each cone to concentrate on the move. Have them try to widen their reach each time. They will reverse the side of the deke when they go through the cones a second time. Take a shot on goal.

LINE C:

Bursts hard up ice, darts puck off boards, cuts around cone and picks the puck up; do not take any shot. Lines A and B must return to their starting lines by skating up the boards nearest Line A; Line C stays at the end of the rink when they have completed their drill; they will return up ice to replicate the move from the other side.

COACHING POINTS:
Switch lines after four minutes.

NAME OF DRILL: All-Skills Puck Control
SKILL TO BE TAUGHT/ENHANCED: Foreskate/Backskate Puck Carry;
One-Hand Rush

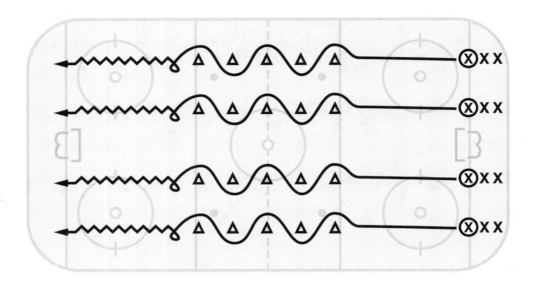

DESCRIPTION OF DRILL:
- Align players at one end of ice as shown.
- On the whistle they will carry the puck with one hand on the stick, cradling it in the crook and angle of the blade.
- Upon reaching the cones, they will resort to two-handed puck control.
- Upon reaching the far blue line they will pivot backward and carry the puck in a backskating mode.
- Repeat the drill back up ice.

COACHING POINTS:
- Generally speaking, five cones in the neutral zone is sufficient to work developmental puck control skills. More than that and it becomes too difficult as there are too many dekes; the drill slows down as kids lose the puck.
- I am hesitant to show young, developmental players the one-handed carry since they will tend to overuse it. Monitor this.

NAME OF DRILL: 3 Drills For The Hands
SKILL TO BE TAUGHT/ENHANCED: Passing: Soft Hands/Quick Hands,
Puck Control
DURATION OF DRILL: 2 min. per station

Drill 1   **Drill 2**   **Drill 3**

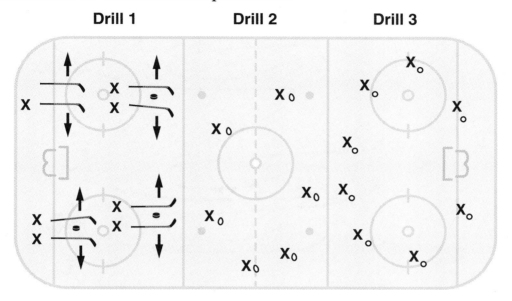

DESCRIPTION OF DRILL:
DRILL #1: TEACHING PASSING AND RECEIVING
Align two players shoulder-to-shoulder. Have them extend their sticks in
a stickhandling mode and place one puck between the sticks. They will
then shuffle the puck back and forth between them mirroring each others' movements.
DRILL #2: TEACHING SOFT HANDS
 Give each player an egg (yes, one bought right from the grocery store!)
and have them shuffle the egg forehand to backhand "giving with hands"
at each touch. Then have them execute a short passing drill, forehand
and backhand, at about 5' distance apart. This will force them to slide
the egg, or puck, rather than slap at it. You saw this drill in the movie
"The Mighty Ducks."
DRILL #3: TEACHING QUICK HANDS
• Use the golf balls written up in the off-ice segment of Volume II. The
   players would work a stationary drill first and then skate with the
   balls, working the ball quickly side-to-side and up ice.
• Younger players just learning to carry the puck seem to get "the feel"
   easier and more quickly. Be sure to have them backskate, too.

NAME OF DRILL: Crazy Eights Drill
SKILL TO BE TAUGHT/ENHANCED: Puck Control, Shooting

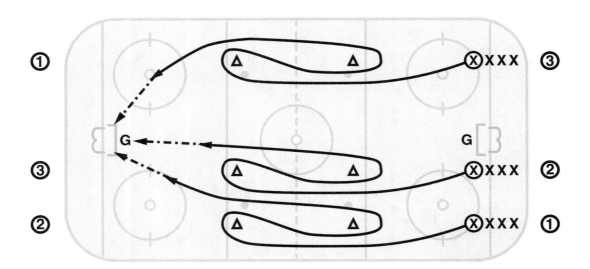

DESCRIPTION OF DRILL:
- Set three lines of players, with pucks, at one end of the ice.
- Use a staggered count and set the lines in motion. The lead skater attacks the cones in a figure-8 pattern and then breaks in for a shot on goal. Have them wait at the shooting end of the ice because ....
- A second trio of three lines will mirror the drill the other way (not shown). This forces the attackers to keep their heads up; the goalies will face many, many shots, too.
- Number each line and work them by command at both ends simultaneously, as shown in the peripheral numbers.

NAME OF DRILL: Perimeter Puck-Control Pivots
SKILL TO BE TAUGHT/ENHANCED: Puck Control

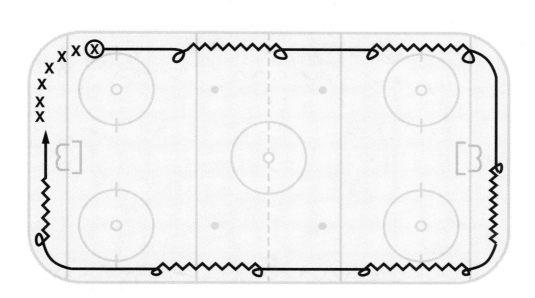

DESCRIPTION OF DRILL:

- This is a simple yet critical drill for intermediate and advanced players to master.
- Simply put, the skaters will circle the perimeter of the ice surface pivoting from foreskating to backskating on each whistle. All the while they must retain control of the puck.
- This is a good team drill. Give each player a puck and have them execute the turns on whistle commands as they skate laps — add knee drops, stops and backskating.

NAME OF DRILL: Escape-N-Go!
SKILL TO BE TAUGHT/ENHANCED: Fighting Through the Check, Stickhandling

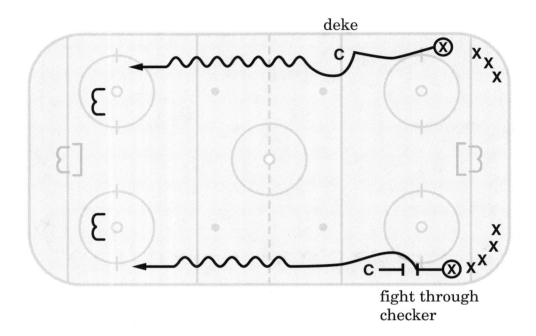

deke

fight through
checker

DESCRIPTION OF DRILL:
- Players are lined up in corners and each has a puck.
- Coach is stationed anywhere between 5' and 15' in front of player who must bull or deke his way through or around the coach who attempts to check the player.
- Coaches may wish to place nets at end of line so that players can add a shot/shooting drill into the overall drill sequence.

COACHING POINTS:
- Drill can be physical for older players.
- The closer the coach is to the player, in terms of his initial alignment, the more physical the drill becomes (i.e., there is less initial room to deke).
- After escaping the check, a passing or stickhandling drill should be incorporated in the neutral zone.

NAME OF DRILL: Two-Man Crab Drill
SKILL TO BE TAUGHT/ENHANCED: Skating Speed, Stickhandling

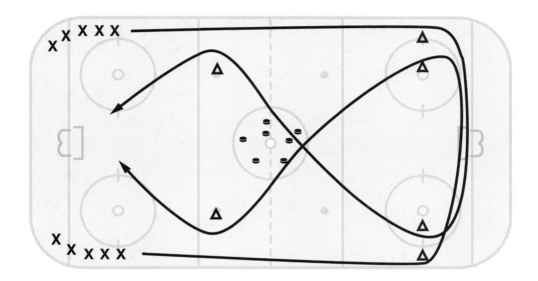

DESCRIPTION OF DRILL:
• This drill can actually be envisioned as a three-step sequence.
• Align players in the end of the rink as shown. On the whistle they will break up ice at full speed weaving through the cones as indicated and accelerating into openings. This skating drill is the first phase.
• In the second sequence, repeat the drill with pucks carried for the entire course of the drill.
• In the third phase, have the players race for pucks lying in the center-ice faceoff circle; the "winner" gets the puck while the "loser" acts as a back-checker attempting to tie up the puck carrier.

COACHING POINTS:
• Coaches may prefer to place just one puck on the center-ice faceoff.
• Also, if a player is trailing too far behind the puck carrier to harry him or her in any way, have them read the shooter's angle and the goalie's rebound angles for a follow-up rebound shot.

NAME OF DRILL: Break-Cut-N-Weave Drill
SKILL TO BE TAUGHT/ENHANCED: Support Pass Receiving, Stickhandling

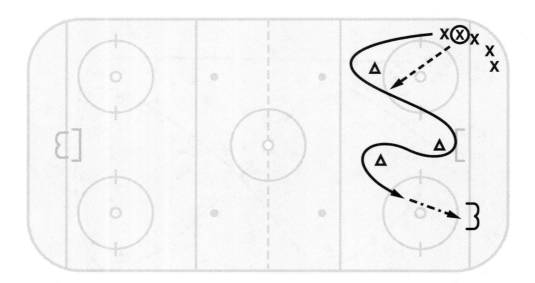

DESCRIPTION OF DRILL:
- Players align in corner as shown.
- On the whistle the player in front breaks up ice and cuts around the cone back toward his line whereupon...
- The second player in line passes the puck to him and then he or she will immediately break as his predecessor did.
- The initial puck carrier weaves through a figure-8 cone arrangement as shown and then takes a shot on goal. (Note the re-positioned net.)
- This drill can be replicated on the other half of the ice to maximize use of the rink surface.

COACHING POINTS:
Make this a hi-tempo drill.

NAME OF DRILL: Teaching Dekes
SKILL TO BE TAUGHT/ENHANCED: Offensive Skills

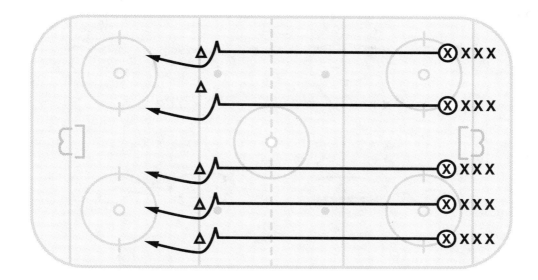

DESCRIPTION OF DRILL:
Offensive attack skills and dekes or "moves" must be isolated, taught and drilled. The Turcotte Stickhandling School does a fine job in doing exactly that. Here is the simple and basic drill they use.
- Teach the group en masse the particular move to be worked, then set players in lines at one end of the ice. They will have a cone or chair in their path somewhere up the ice.
- On the whistle, the lead player breaks for the cone and executes the move to a predetermined side.
- Repeat to the other side and work each move that you wish to impart in a similar mirrored way.

COACHING POINTS:
Teach the following moves at least:
- Wide dekes: in/out
- Head fake: drive off the skate to the fake side
- Slip-thru: quick hands
- Pull-in: show puck and take away same
- Fake shot and go: top speed
- Spin move

NAME OF DRILL: Four-Corner Deke Drill
SKILL TO BE TAUGHT/ENHANCED: Stickhandling

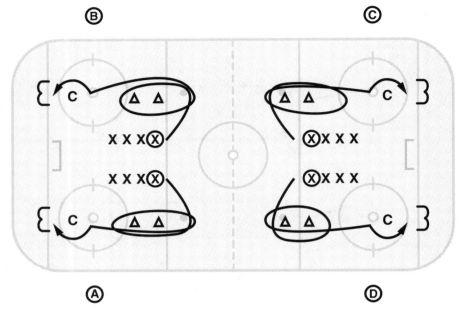

DESCRIPTION OF DRILL:
Dekes must be taught. That is the purpose of this four-station drill. To begin each drill, the skater accelerates around the cones as shown and then attacks a live but stationary "dummy" coach standing in tripod positioning.

DRILL STATION A:
"Take-away" by faking one side with good head and shoulder fake, emphasizing the wide extension of the stick, and slipping around the coach.

DRILL STATION B:
"Power Move" around the coach by deking to the forehand side, sliding the puck around the backhand and placing the body between the coach (checker) and the puck. Drop the inside arm down to the ice as a shield. Keep the puck at short-arm's length on the hip.

DRILL STATION C:
Fake the shot and slip the puck around the coach to the forehand or backhand side. Use a fake slapshot.

DRILL STATION D:
"Spin move" around the coach with a "showing" of the puck on the forehand side and then a tight hockey turn around the coach/checker.

Each station needs to be only 3-5 minutes in length.

NAME OF DRILL: Pivot and Break Drill
SKILL TO BE TAUGHT/ENHANCED: Backskating Puck Control,
Breakaway Creativity

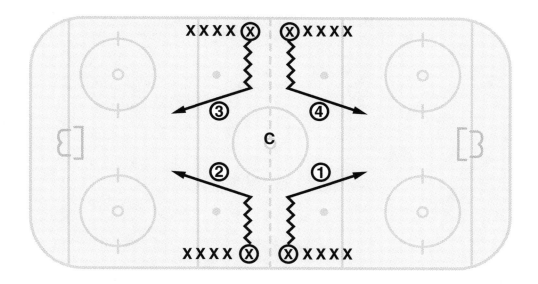

DESCRIPTION OF DRILL:
- Set four lines of players in the neutral zone along the board as shown.
  The coach in the middle merely directs traffic by yelling out the num-
  ber of each line in sequence.
- On each command, the lead player in the line called out will backskate,
  quickly accelerating, with a puck until he/she hears a whistle to pivot
  into the foreskate mode for a breakaway on the goalie.
- Look for a specific move on each breakaway.

NAME OF DRILL: Quick Feet/Quick Hands Drill
SKILL TO BE TAUGHT/ENHANCED: Stickhandling, Agility

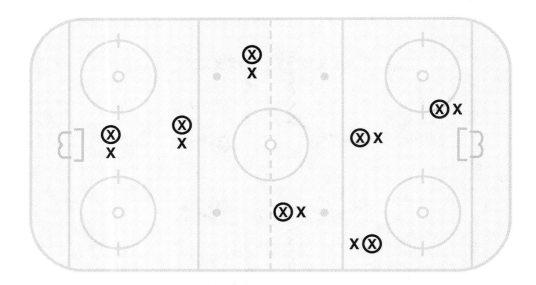

DESCRIPTION OF DRILL:
- Pair your players up and place them at various spots on the ice.
- One player is standing with his stick in his hands and a puck at his or her midline.
- The other player is kneeling with their stick just off the ice and off to the side of the erect player's skates.
- On the whistle the erect player begins a side-to-side dribble with the puck. The kneeling player will proceed to swing his/her stick side-to-side and force the dribbling player to hop over the swinging stick while dribbling the puck at the same time.

NAME OF DRILL: "Chaos!" Drill
SKILL TO BE TAUGHT/ENHANCED: Hi-Speed Skating with Pucks

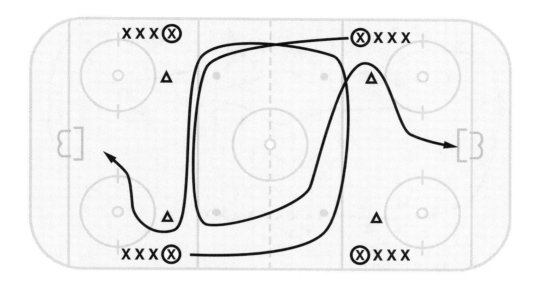

DESCRIPTION OF DRILL:
- Align four groups of players in areas along the boards and blue lines as shown.
- This drill can be done with four players breaking at once or on staggered whistles. Bear in mind that one of the components of this drill is to emphasize speed, puck control and keeping the head up. The closer the whistles are together, or the more simultaneous the breaking players are, the more the "head-up" aspect is highlighted.
- Only two routes are shown for the sake of clarity in depicting the drill, but all four groups will skate a mirrored pattern.
- Conclude each skaters' route with a shot on goal.

COACHING POINTS:
- Note that the neutral zone faceoff dots are employed to help outline the skating route.
- You may wish to have only two diagonally opposite players break at the same time (as shown).

NAME OF DRILL: Run The Gauntlet (II)
SKILL TO BE TAUGHT/ENHANCED: Stickhandling, Passing Accuracy

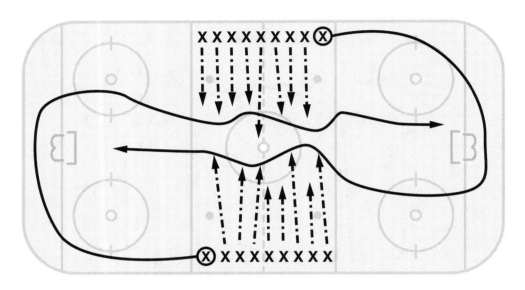

DESCRIPTION OF DRILL:
Players at the beginning of each line will carry into zone, around net and through the neutral zone. However, once they hit the neutral zone, they will be shot at (puck must stay on the ice!) by teammates along boards and in line. Shooters are attempting to knock the puck off handlers' sticks.

NAME OF DRILL: Slow Skate/Fast Puck Drill
SKILL TO BE TAUGHT/ENHANCED: Stickhandling

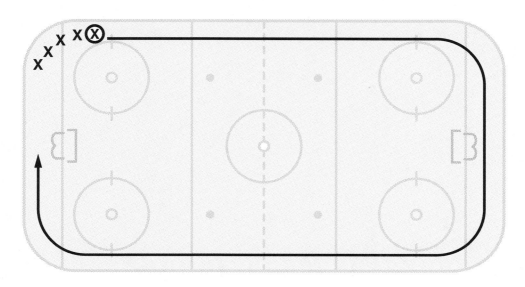

DESCRIPTION OF DRILL:
- In this drill, which is admittedly difficult, players will circle the ice with a puck and stick. Their goal is to learn to play the puck off their own skates while in motion. Except to accelerate, they are to keep their skates on the ice at all times and work the puck off inside and outside edges, angle-deflecting the puck on and off their stick.
- For example, with one hand on the stick, tap the puck on to the outside edge of a lead skate and angle the deflection forward. Or, tap the puck off a lagging back skate and back up and out on to the stick.

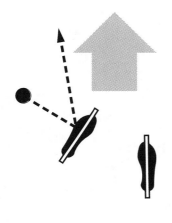

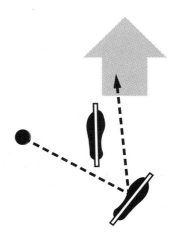

PASSING DRILLS

— INSTRUCTIONAL DRILLS
—SPECIALIZED PASSES
— INTERMEDIATE-LEVEL PASSING DRILLS

"Pass from the heart."

Slava Fetisov
World-Class Soviet
Defenseman

NAME OF DRILL: 2 and 3-Man Stationary Passing
SKILL TO BE TAUGHT/ENHANCED: Forehand/Backhand Passing

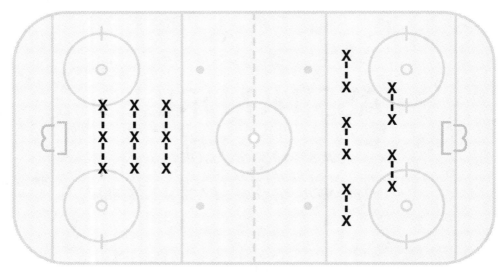

Three Man   **Two Man**

DESCRIPTION OF DRILL:

2–MAN DRILL:

Align your players in teams of two and set them up by facing each of them up ice in the same direction. They will slide the puck back and forth between them on the whistle.

3–MAN DRILL:

- Set your players up in trios and repeat the same drill described above. Be sure to rotate the players.
- Be sure to monitor the players in terms of the direction they face. Younger players will want to turn to face their partner; they may want to walk around their backhand, too.

COACHING POINTS:

A good variation off the 3-man passing drill is to spread the trio out and have the two end players attempt to flip the puck while the middle man works on knock-downs to gain control.

NAME OF DRILL: Instructional Flip Passing
SKILL TO BE TAUGHT/ENHANCED: Flip Passing Over A Checker's Stick

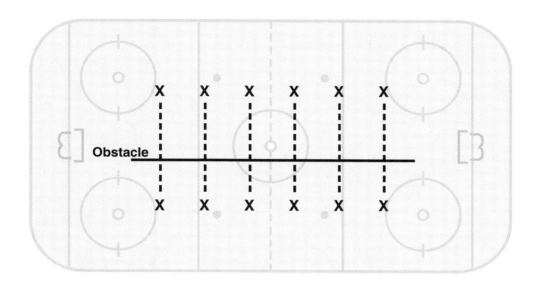

DESCRIPTION OF DRILL:
- Several different types of obstacles can be used in this drill: stick, a "stick rope,"* flattened folding chairs or a fire hose.
- Align the players in pairs facing each other on either side of the obstacle and have them, while stationary, flip pass the puck over the obstacle.
- More advanced players can do this drill as a 2-0 skating the length of the ice on either side of the obstacle.
- More advanced players should also be taught the backhand flip pass, too.

COACHING POINTS:
- Use the alignment of this drill to teach the basics of forehand/backhand passing first! No rope, firehose, or other obstacle should be used in teaching the basics at first.
- Teach the players to lift the puck yet allow it to land flat. To do this properly, have the players set the puck on the heel of their stickblades and "slice" it toward the receiver. Young players all too often try to "scoop" the puck, and this causes it to bounce and roll.

*How to make a "stick-rope" is described on page 57 in this volume.

NAME OF DRILL: Instructional Board Passing
SKILL TO BE TAUGHT/ENHANCED: Use of Boards in Passing
DURATION OF DRILL: 2-4 mins.

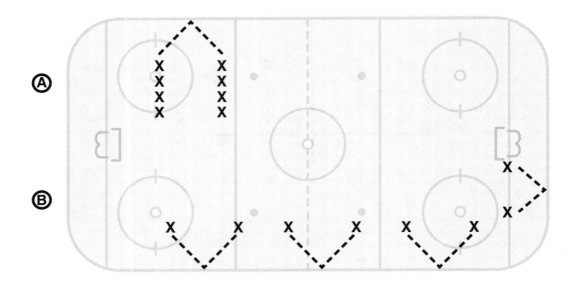

DESCRIPTION OF DRILL:
- Set players in pairs in either way indicated above,(a) or (b), depending upon how much ice surface you have to work with.
- After having taught the sweep-pass technique, teach the young players the proper angle and have them work board passes to each other.

COACHING POINTS:
- In drill format (b), the players pass to each other and then rotate to the back of the line and switch sides.
- Keep the paired players away from the rounded corners since the angle reads will be nonexistent.
- Advanced players can use drill format (a) and perform the drill as they skate around the ice surface perimeter using both fore- and backskating.

NAME OF DRILL: Mobile Board Passing
SKILL TO BE TAUGHT/ENHANCED: Lead Passes, Drop Passes Off Boards

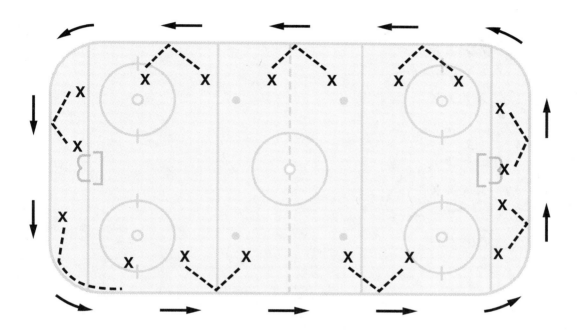

DESCRIPTION OF DRILL:
- Players will skate in pairs about 10' apart. They will circle around the rink lead-passing and back-passing off the boards.
- After a lap or two, have the players face each other so that one is backskating while the other is foreskating, repeating the same drill. Have them switch positioning halfway around the rink.

NAME OF DRILL: Board Pass-Shot Drill
SKILL TO BE TAUGHT/ENHANCED: Board-Passing, Shooting

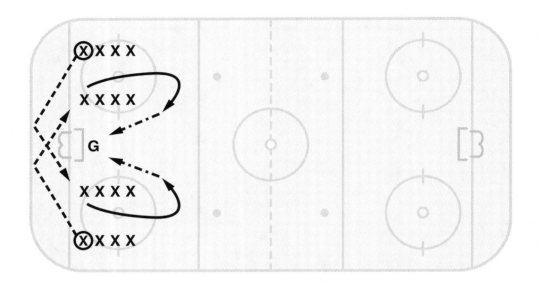

DESCRIPTION OF DRILL:
- Align four groups of players as shown. Be careful to set them on the dots and hashmarks as indicated. They also will set up along the goalline. Each line has pucks. A goalie is in the net.
- On command, one of the outside lines will pass the puck off the backboards to one of the inside lines. The pass receiver wheels to the outside of the line and attacks the net for a close-in shot on goal.
- Repeat with other lines passing in sequence. Also, be sure to use the inside lines to pass to the outside lines, too.
- The goalies can benefit from this drill by facing up ice and reacting across the crease to skaters breaking in suddenly from either direction.
- Until the players learn the pattern to the drill, call out numbers designated for each line.

COACHING POINTS:
- Emphasize backhand and forehand passing as well as shooting.
- Use both ends of the ice simultaneously.

NAME OF DRILL: Backskate/Foreskate Passing
SKILL TO BE TAUGHT/ENHANCED: Puck Control, Passing in Motion

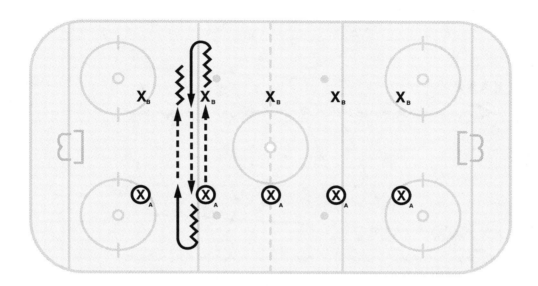

DESCRIPTION OF DRILL:
- To maximize the ice surface on this drill, work it the width of the rink. Have players set up in pairs at mid-ice about 12-15' apart. Player A has puck and foreskates toward player B who is backskating. As soon as A releases the puck, he is to backskate and receive pass from B who is now coming at him. At each pass, the sequence of foreskate/backskate changes for each player.
- The drill assumes a linear pattern, but what is diagrammed is a drifting pattern only for the sake of clarity in diagramming the drill.

NAME OF DRILL: Foreskate/Backskate Passing
SKILL TO BE TAUGHT/ENHANCED: Passing While Skating Forward
and Backward

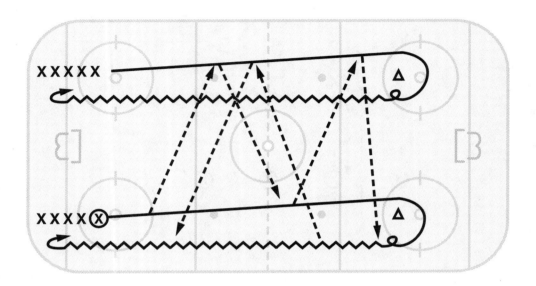

DESCRIPTION OF DRILL:
- Align players in 2 lines for a simple 2-0.
- When they reach the cones, they will turn and backskate, yet still passing 2-0.

COACHING POINTS:
All too often players of all levels slap their passes; work on having them
slide the puck.

NAME OF DRILL: Drop Pass Drill I
SKILL TO BE TAUGHT/ENHANCED: Drop Pass

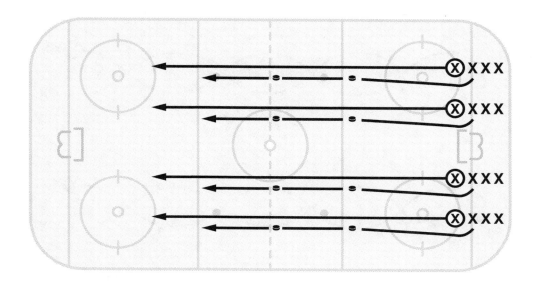

DESCRIPTION OF DRILL:
- Set lines of players up in groups of four or five as shown. The line leader has a puck.
- After having taught the technique of the drop pass (i.e., stickblade tapped in front of puck's travel line to stop it), have the lead player carry to the blue line, and drop pass it. The next player on line, having skated on a second whistle, picks it up and carries to either the red line or the opposite blue line. The next player in line breaks on the next whistle and picks up the dropped puck, carrying it to the next line to drop pass it for the next player.

COACHING POINTS:
Make the drill competitive — check to see that each puck dropped is indeed resting on the line called for. This will often be difficult, so reward the team who has the most successfully precise drops.

NAME OF DRILL: Drop Passes II: Cut-N-Weave
SKILL TO BE TAUGHT/ENHANCED: Offensive Pattern Play, Drop Passes

Line-Set No. 1

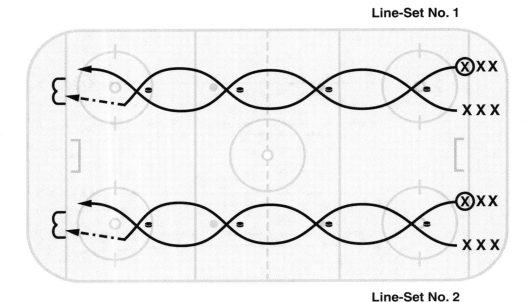

Line-Set No. 2

DESCRIPTION OF DRILL:
- Set up four lines of players at one end of ice. Players are to be paired up in two line-sets with one skater having a puck.
- On the whistle the first two players in each line will begin a weave sequence with the lead player drop-passing the puck to the player cutting behind.

COACHING POINTS:
Set both nets at one end of the ice and have the line-sets finish with a shot on goal.

NAME OF DRILL: Three-Drop Drill
SKILL TO BE TAUGHT/ENHANCED: Drop Passing

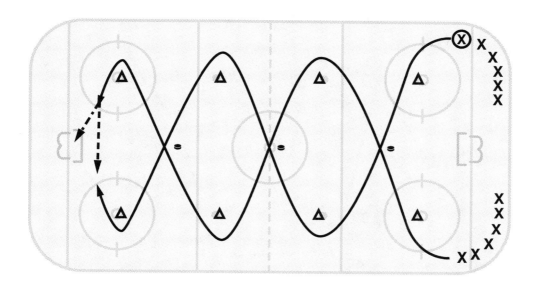

DESCRIPTION OF DRILL:
- Line the skaters in the corners and along the backline. On the whistle, the leading two players will break around the first cone, set on the faceoff dot as shown. One player has a puck and he/she will lay a drop pass in the middle.
- The other player will pick up the puck and as they weave down the ice, each time their paths cross, a drop pass is to be set.
- Note that there is a cone on each dot; this will result in three drop passes.
- Finish the drill with a shot on goal.

NAME OF DRILL: Stationary Keep-Away
SKILL TO BE TAUGHT/ENHANCED: Passing

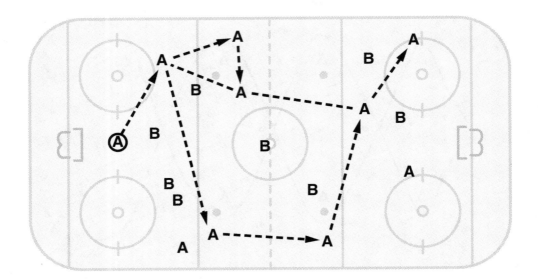

DESCRIPTION OF DRILL:
- Can use full ice or zones.
- Scatter players on team A randomly about the zone or ice. Team B's players must try to steal the puck — they can skate after it. Team A has possession, but they must stay still and only propel the puck by hard, sharp passes.
- When Team B steals the puck, they will freeze and Team A attempts to pick off the pass.

COACHING POINTS:
- Teach the team attempting to steal the puck to read the passer's eyes. This is a good forechecking technique.
- Flip passes and one-timed tap passes can be employed by more advanced players.

NAME OF DRILL: Clearing and Knockdown Drill
SKILL TO BE TAUGHT/ENHANCED: Clearing Pucks From Defensive
End, Controlling Airborne and Bouncing Pucks

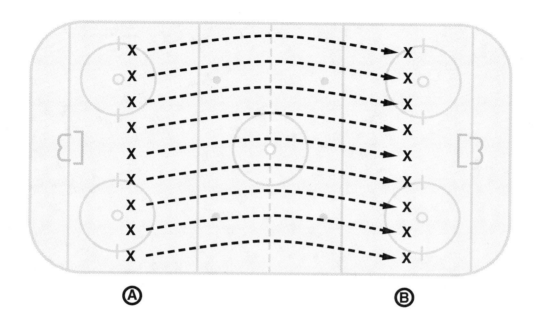

DESCRIPTION OF DRILL:
- This drill can be done off-ice, too. In addition, it can be done as a "warm-down" drill for a team fatigued from higher-tempo skating drills performed earlier in a practice. Nevertheless, this drill incorporates necessary, not to mention forgotten, skills.
- Line A lofts a high clearing "pass" down the ice. Teach the proper technique of toe-control, high follow-through and "pitching hay" styles. The puck should come down somewhere in the neighborhood of a player on Line B. It should be bouncing or even airborne. Line B must control control it and loft it back to Line A.
- Work the backhand, too.

NAME OF DRILL: Puck-Flung Drill
SKILL TO BE TAUGHT/ENHANCED: Controlling/Stopping the Pass
Flung Around the Boards

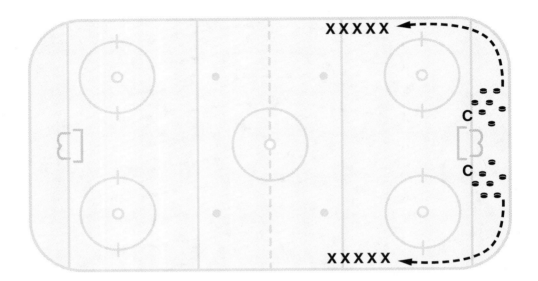

DESCRIPTION OF DRILL:
- This is largely an instructional drill and both ends of the ice with four corners can be used.
- Coaches will fling the puck sharply and with hard speed around the boards as shown. They may send it high off the glass or swiftly along the edgeboards.
- The players must control the pass which is more often than not a dump-out clear by the opposition. Teach proper body position and skate angles as well as the notion of "gloving" the puck and setting it down.

NAME OF DRILL: Traditional Give-N-Go Drill
SKILL TO BE TAUGHT/ENHANCED: Elementary Passing Skills

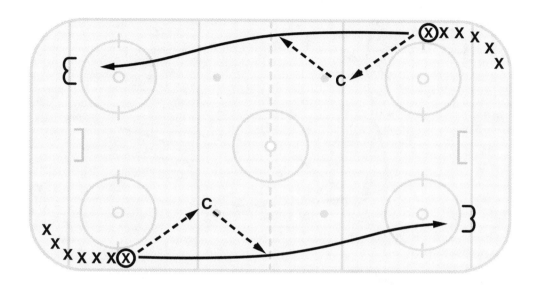

DESCRIPTION OF DRILL:
• Divide rink in half with lines of players in opposite corners and nets set up at base of circles as shown.
• Teach the elements of passing and pass receiving.
• The players will pass to the coach at the blue line, break into the neutral zone for a pass, receive it and then either stickhandle through cones or shoot on goal.

COACHING POINTS:
• Players must learn to pass hard, give with the puck when receiving it (or take it off the boards when they miss it), and break into full stride, with stickblade on ice, to receive the return pass.
• Young players will often slow down after passing. Furthermore, they will fail to place their blade on the ice when requesting the return pass.

NAME OF DRILL: Hard Cuts Give-N-Go Drill
SKILL TO BE TAUGHT/ENHANCED: Skating, Passing, Shooting

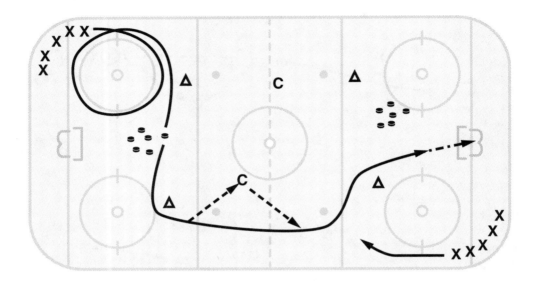

DESCRIPTION OF DRILL:
- A full-ice drill, align the players in the corner. On the whistle they will break, accelerating as they go, around their near faceoff circle.
- After skating the circle, the player will pick up a puck in the near slot, break around a cone and execute a give-n-go with a player or coach in the neutral zone.
- The player will then skate in for a shot on goal.
- Replicate the drill going the other way, but only after the players learn the traffic pattern.

COACHING POINTS:
Note that the cones are set at angles that force sharp breaks both on the pass and after receiving it. The latter forces a sharp-turn "drive" to the net.

NAME OF DRILL: Escape, Give-N-Go
SKILL TO BE TAUGHT/ENHANCED: Stickhandling, Passing, Receiving

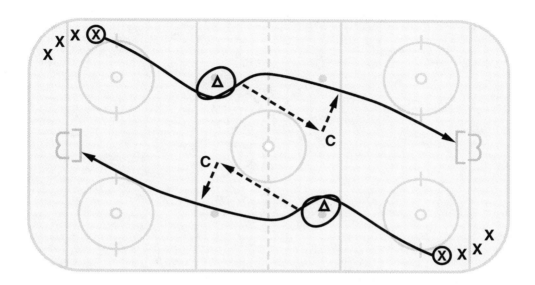

DESCRIPTION OF DRILL:

- Players align in two lines in opposite corners.
- Utilize one-handed carry to a cone, use two hands on stick to circle and escape cone (i.e., the "checker") and then...
- Break through the neutral zone employing a give-n-go with a stationary coach.
- Finish with a shot on goal.

COACHING POINTS:

An interesting variation of this simple drill is to simply move the cone closer to the boards, about five feet out from them, and have the player tap a pass off the boards to himself before breaking for the give-n-go.

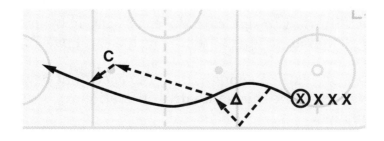

NAME OF DRILL: Circle Passing Drill
SKILL TO BE TAUGHT/ENHANCED: Elements of Passing, Pass Receiving

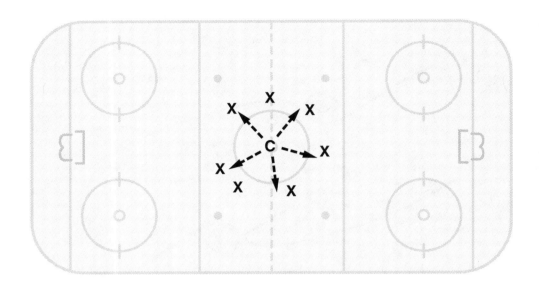

DESCRIPTION OF DRILL:
- Place a coach with 2 pucks at the center of each faceoff circle. Standing around and along the perimeter of each circle is a group of players.
- The coach will pass the puck rapidly to each of the players (the second puck he has is only a spare when the passed puck is misplayed). Make this a rapid-fire drill; only the coach is allowed to one-time the pass, unless, of course, you would wish to emphasize the teaching and drilling of this skill.
- The wily coach can at times let a hard pass to him slip through to an unsuspecting player behind him or her, too. A skilled coach can tap-pass or deflect the passes to "sleeping" players, also.

COACHING POINTS:
- The players must keep their sticks on the ice and be looking for the puck at all times.
- The players will want to replicate the coach's style by one-timing and tap passing. If you are trying to teach the basics of passing and receiving, do not allow them to do this.
- If the players are skilled enough, take the coach out of the circle and have the players work this same drill in stationary, foreskating and backskating modes.

NAME OF DRILL: Tic-Tac-Toe Drill
SKILL TO BE TAUGHT/ENHANCED: Touch-Passing, Quick Passes

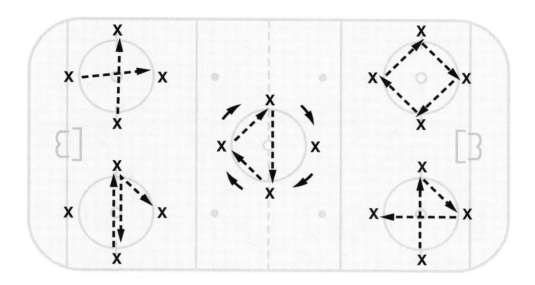

DESCRIPTION OF DRILL:
- Align players in groups of four along perimeter of each circle.
- On the whistle they are to tap-pass, or touch-pass, the puck across the circle as quickly as possible. Durations of only 10-20 seconds are necessary. Have the players count passes to foster a bit of competition between the groups.
- More skilled teams can have the players execute this drill in motion as they skate around the perimeter of the circles (shown in center ice circle).

NAME OF DRILL: Escape-N-Pass I
SKILL TO BE TAUGHT/ENHANCED: Tight Turns, Passing, Escapes, Support

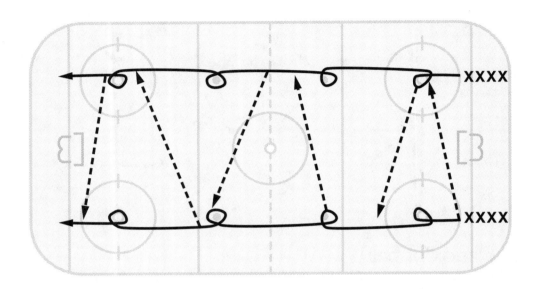

DESCRIPTION OF DRILL:
- Line the players up at the end of the rink as shown.
- This drill is a 2-0 passing drill going the length of the ice, but it has the additional element of employing tight hockey turns performed at each of the four faceoff dots, passing, breaking into the opening, and locating the puck carrier.
- The players should visualize this drill in terms of escaping a checker, supporting the puck carrier by breaking into the opening up ice, and locating the puck carrier after coming off an escape.

COACHING POINTS:
Have the players perform all of their turns to the inside of the ice surface so that when they switch lines to come back up ice, they will have worked their other turn-side, not to mention the backhand to forehand change.

NAME OF DRILL: Escape-and-Pass II
SKILL TO BE TAUGHT/ENHANCED: Puck Control and Quick Passing

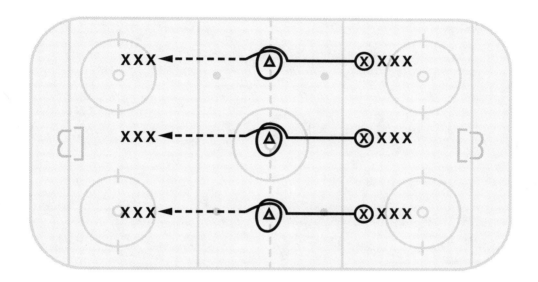

DESCRIPTION OF DRILL:
• Line players facing each other in the neutral zone with cone along the redline as shown.
• As the whistle sounds, have the player with a puck break for the cone, spin into an escape move (with a tight hockey turn around the cone to a predetermined side) and then immediately pass off.
• The pass receiver then breaks for the cones to mirror the drill.

COACHING POINTS:
Be sure to control, by signaling, the side to which they turn so that you can ensure the mirrored skill.

NAME OF DRILL: Corner-Point Passing
SKILL TO BE TAUGHT/ENHANCED: Coordination Between Wing in
Corner and Point

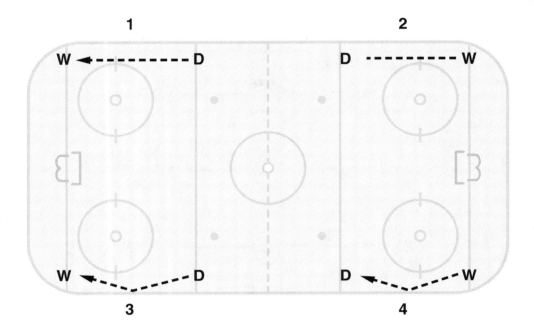

DESCRIPTION OF DRILL:
- Work all four corners at same time.
- Four passes must be completed before a shot is taken:
  — D passes directly to W and then W passes back to D.
  — D board-passes to W and W board-passes to D. Player D can either
    slap/snap shoot or "walk in;" W should break for post to tip it in.

COACHING POINTS:
This is a more advanced form of the "Tip-In Drill" described on page 144.

NAME OF DRILL: 10-Pass 2-0
SKILL TO BE TAUGHT/ENHANCED: Passing Skills

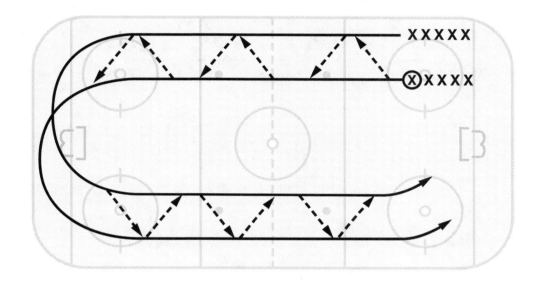

DESCRIPTION OF DRILL:

• Align players in 2 lines near corner.
• Skate down one lane passing 2-on-0; switch lanes and return up other side of ice.
• The goal is for 10 passes, but more advanced players can work to complete 15 or even 20 passes; tap-passes can be employed by the more advanced skaters to accomplish this goal.

NAME OF DRILL: 2-0 Stop-N-Go
SKILL TO BE TAUGHT/ENHANCED: Passing with evasive element

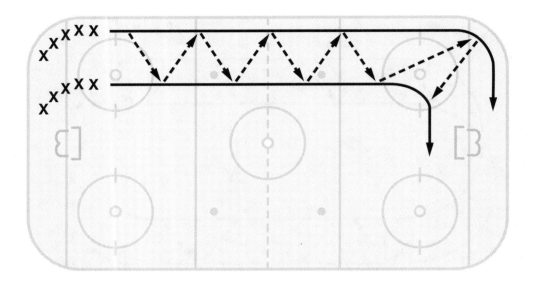

DESCRIPTION OF DRILL:
- Players will circle the ice executing a simple 2-on-0 passing drill,but there is a twist. When a player receives the pass, he/she must abruptly stop before returning the pass.
- This drill teaches a certain evasive measure against a checker, an often forgotten element. It also teaches the pass receiver to break after passing off.

NAME OF DRILL: "88" 2-on-0 Drill
SKILL TO BE TAUGHT/ENHANCED: Skating, Passing

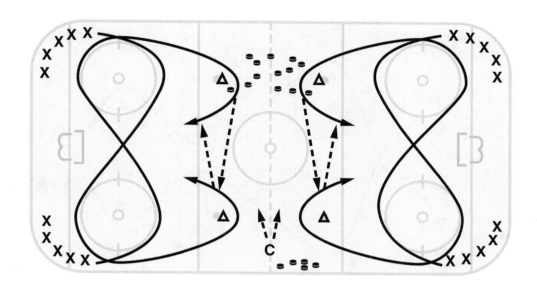

DESCRIPTION OF DRILL:
- Simultaneously executed at both ends of the rink, the name the drill derives from the figure-8 patterns which end up being 2-on-0 passing patterns.
- Line the players up in the corners. On the whistle all four players will break around the top of the endzone faceoff circle, cross to the other circle skating along the bottom and outside rim, break into the neutral zone and around the cone as shown and then meet up with the player mirroring the drill for a 2-on-0 attack on the goal.
- Pucks are either picked up in the neutral zone as shown or received from a coach waiting to pass.

NAME OF DRILL: 2-0 Variation Passing Drill
SKILL TO BE TAUGHT/ENHANCED: Passing

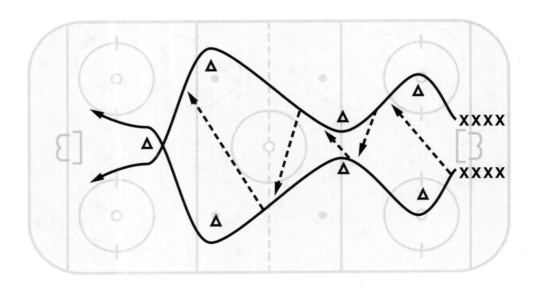

DESCRIPTION OF DRILL:
- Conceptually, this drill teaches players to break wide for outlet passes, utilize support concepts to come back toward the carrier, as well as drop passes, crossing patterns and tap-passes.
- The tap-passes, or one-timed passes, should be used in the narrow bottleneck as shown. The drop pass should be utilized at the cone on the far end by the shooting net.

NAME OF DRILL: 2-on-0 Bob-N-Weave Drill
SKILL TO BE TAUGHT/ENHANCED: Passing, Heads-up Puck Control

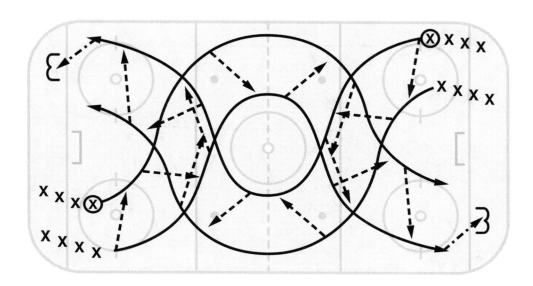

DESCRIPTION OF DRILL:
- This is a simple 2-on-0 drill made more difficult by sending out four players, two from each end simultaneously.
- The pairs must weave through the circles as shown. They can incorporate tap-passes, drop passes, and so forth, but they had better keep their heads up!
- Finish with a shot on goal in nets that are repositioned as shown.

NAME OF DRILL: Wide 'N' Narrow Passing Drill
SKILL TO BE TAUGHT/ENHANCED: Passing

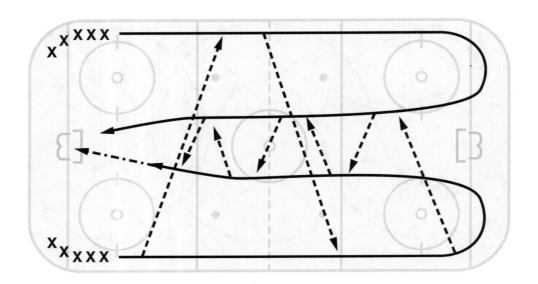

DESCRIPTION OF DRILL:
- Players will align in the corners as shown and execute a series of hard, crisp bullet passes across ice to "wide wings" as they break down the ice toward the far circles.
- Upon reaching the circles, they will peel back toward their own goal executing a series of tap-passes until they are within shooting range.

NAME OF DRILL: Transitional 2-on-0
SKILL TO BE TAUGHT/ENHANCED: 2-0 Passing, Backchecking

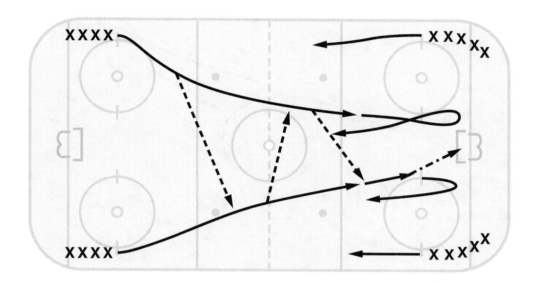

DESCRIPTION OF DRILL:
- Begin with 2-0 up ice and shot is taken.
- Attacker will then slap goalpost with his stick to signal next set of 2 skaters to begin their 2-0.
- Attackers who have just shot will then chase next set of 2-0 attackers down the ice in attempt to foil.

NAME OF DRILL: Buttonhook-N-Breakout Pass
SKILL TO BE TAUGHT/ENHANCED: Passing, Defensive Zone Breakouts, Shooting

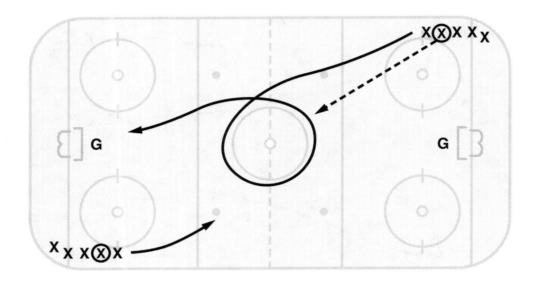

DESCRIPTION OF DRILL:
- Players skate hard from hashmarks to center-ice circle.
- Second player in line passes the puck to the first skater once he has "buttonhooked" back to his blue line. The passer then breaks for the circle.
- Meanwhile, the pass receiver now breaks into the offensive zone for a shot on goal. (Only one side is diagrammed for the sake of clarity, but the lines on either side should alternately go.)

NAME OF DRILL: Circle In
SKILL TO BE TAUGHT/ENHANCED: Skating, Passing, Shooting

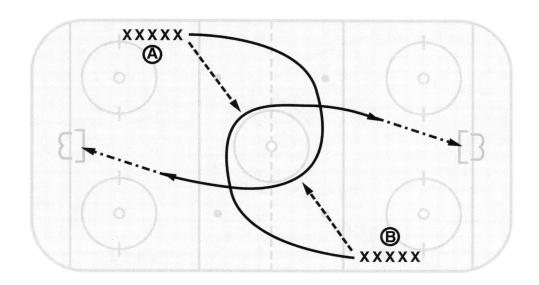

DESCRIPTION OF DRILL:
• Divide players into two groups along sideboards opposite each other.
• Lead player in Line A breaks into neutral zone and receives pass from lead skater in Line B who then immediately breaks into neutral zone for a pass from Line A.
• Players switch lines after they have taken shot.

COACHING POINTS:
• Use goalies or shooting boards.
• Make this a high-tempo drill.

NAME OF DRILL: Cross-Body Passing Drill
SKILL TO BE TAUGHT/ENHANCED: Tactical Passing

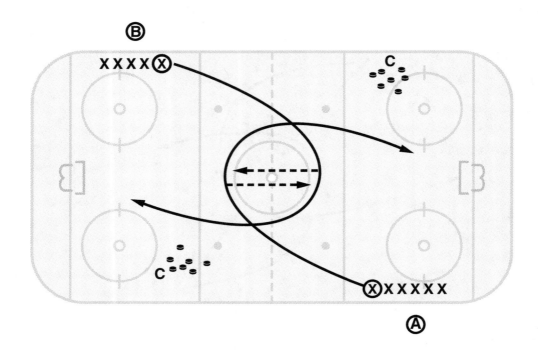

DESCRIPTION OF DRILL:
- Align players along boards as shown, each leader with a puck.
- On the whistle, they both break for the center-ice circle where each will deliver a cross-body pass as shown.
- One pass each is all that is immediately necessary, but since this is a difficult drill, several passes will miss their mark. Keep coaches with spare pucks in the vicinity so the skaters can finish the drill with a shot on goal.

COACHING POINTS:
- This is a complex drill so you may wish to begin with one designated line carrying one puck before progressing to two pucks.
- Teach the soft pass since the cross-body pass, notwithstanding its cross-under hands passing technique, is a timing pass which should meet with the skater at a particular spot. This drill also teaches the players to pass to a spot, thereby allowing the receiver to "catch up to it."

NAME OF DRILL: Problem Passes Drill
SKILL TO BE TAUGHT/ENHANCED: Receiving problem passes too far in front or too close in on skates

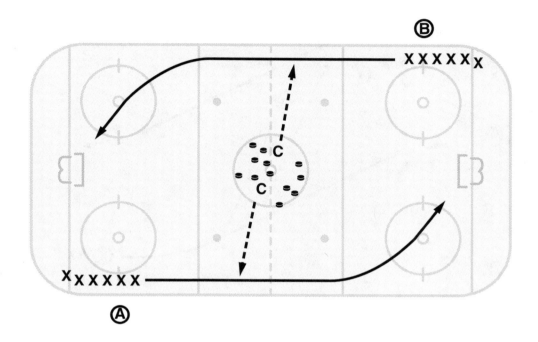

DESCRIPTION OF DRILL:
- Align players in corners as shown. Players in Line A will attempt to receive a pass which is just beyond their reach. Teach them to "dead stick" it by reaching out with one hand or to drop to a knee and hook the puck.
- Players in Line B will take a close-in pass off their skates by angling and deflecting the puck off their skate blades and on to their stick.
- Coaches skilled in passing will align with pucks in the center-ice circle.

NAME OF DRILL: Two-Man Pass-N-Shoot
SKILL TO BE TAUGHT/ENHANCED: Passing, Attacking Net, Shooting

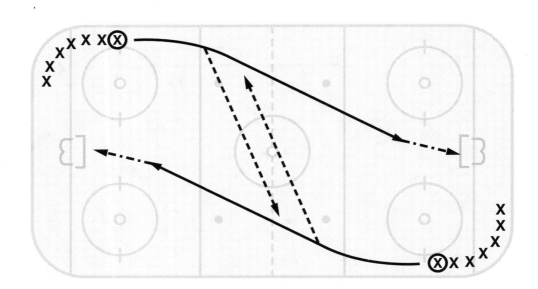

DESCRIPTION OF DRILL:
- Align players in opposite corners as shown. Each line has pucks.
- On the whistle, the first two players in each line will break toward center ice, but when they hit the blue line, they will pass, hard and on the fly, to their opposite-lined partner.
- The pass receivers break toward the net for a shot on goal.

COACHING POINTS:
- The higher the level of play, the more players need to learn to pass the puck hard, sharply and crisply "on to the tape." This drill can be as easy or as difficult as the coach chooses to make it, and this is all based on the speed of passing.
- A key concept to impart here is that of "anticipatory passing" or sliding the puck to where the receiver will be rather than where he/she is when the passer first sees him or her.

NAME OF DRILL: "Loops" Drill
SKILL TO BE TAUGHT/ENHANCED: High-speed Passing, Cycling

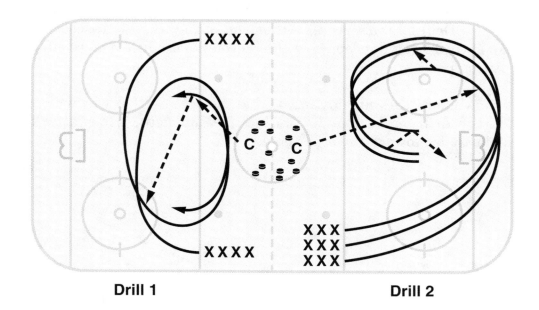

Drill 1   **Drill 2**

DESCRIPTION OF DRILL:
Two drills are described here and both are for more advanced players in
a high-tempo pace. They are primarily designed for forwards.
DRILL #1:
Align the players along the boards as shown; coach stands in middle
along the red line with pucks. On the whistle, a player from each line
breaks into the zone in a looping manner across the top of the faceoff
circles. One of them receives a pass from the coach. They continue their
loop by returning to the neutral zone and then attacking the offensive
zone once again, all the while employing quick passes as in a 2-0 sce-
nario.
DRILL #2:
Set all three lines of players along one side of the neutral zone boards
near a blue line. On the whistle, all three players break into the zone,
slicing across one circle and along the base of the far circle.* At that
point the coach passes to one of the players and a 3-0 ensues as they
cycle out of the zone and back in to attack the net.

COACHING POINTS:

The players should envision this drill as follows: the first loop into the zone is that of "support" in that they are coming back into the defensive zone. The second loop calls for them to attack, hence the zone is now an offensive one. Use the term "regroup" for this drill. Also, should you prefer to use Drill #2 mirrored at either end of the ice, set the coach with pucks at the faceoff dots opposite the regroup to produce a more effective transition pass.

* As shown here, they are circling behind the net — either way will work. Also, this drill can be done in a full-ice fashion as the trio of attackers breaks up ice toward the other goal.

NAME OF DRILL: Trio-Rush Drill
SKILL TO BE TAUGHT/ENHANCED: Skating, Shooting, Passing and
Combo Play

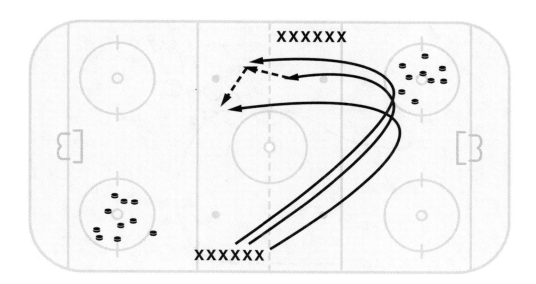

DESCRIPTION OF DRILL:
- Scatter loose pucks in the endzone faceoff circles and align the players along the neutral zone boards, as shown.
- Work both ends of the ice simultaneously.
- On the whistle, the first three players in each line will break for the far end of the ice where one will pick up a loose puck and initiate a 3-0 rush which will end in shots on goal.

NAME OF DRILL: Double-Tap Passing Drill
SKILL TO BE TAUGHT/ENHANCED: Passing-tap, One-timed, Touch-passes

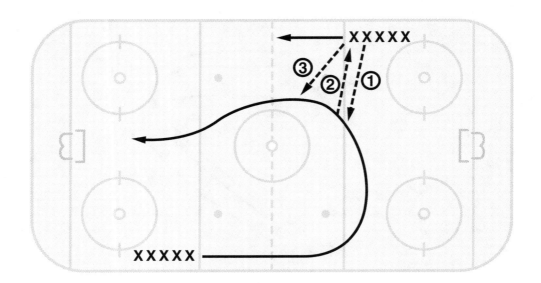

DESCRIPTION OF DRILL:
Players align near the boards as shown. The lead player, on the whistle, breaks for the far neutral zone faceoff dot, skims the blue line to the center-ice faceoff circle as indicated. He or she receives a pass from the lead person on the opposite line. The pass is tapped back and forth once each and then the recipient breaks into the offensive zone for a shot on goal. Once the original passer has tapped a one-timed pass to the at-tacker, he/she then breaks on a mirrored pattern to replicate the drill from the opposite side.

COACHING POINTS:
• In teaching the tap-pass, make sure that the passer and receiver have the stick blade facing each other. There is a slight stiffening to the lower hand and wrist in executing this pass, too.
• As the players tire in this drill, there will be a tendency to widen the gap between the passers. Keep them close, preferably within 15 feet.

SHOOTING DRILLS

"Sure I work them hard. I don't want my players coming back a year later saying that we could have won a national championship if I'd worked them harder."

Coach Joe Paterno

NAME OF DRILL: 3-Station Shooting Instruction
SKILL TO BE TAUGHT/ENHANCED: Wrist, Backhand, One-timed Shots.
DURATION OF DRILL: 5 min. per station

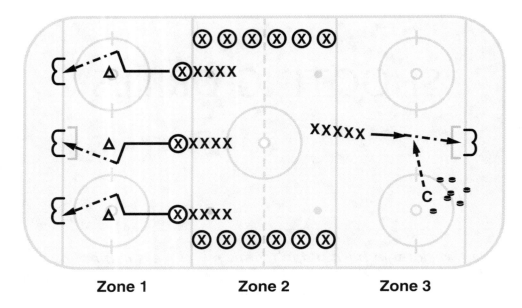

Zone 1   **Zone 2**   **Zone 3**

DESCRIPTION OF DRILL:
- Players in Zone 1 are learning the backhand shot by attacking a cone, deking to their backhand and shooting with proper hand spacing and weight transfer.
- Players in Zone 2 are learning to pull the puck from their rear skate,* shifting weight from back foot to front foot, rolling the bottom hand over and following through to the target in the wrist shot. You may even wish to draw on the boards with a dry-marker pen so the players have a target.
- Players in Zone 3 are learning to one-time the shot. Coaches will slide the puck gently across the shooter's path. Have them pre-position their weight and stick so they they can "drive through the puck" when shooting this. Although the one-timer is a somewhat advanced shot, it is important for players to learn that a quick release is essential. This teaches that. For the youngest players, I literally sit on the ice and slide a puck to them by hand.

*Young players almost always shoot with the puck on the front foot unless otherwise taught.

NAME OF DRILL: Shooting and Goalie Warmup Drill
SKILL TO BE TAUGHT/ENHANCED: Skating, Shooting, Goalie Set-ups

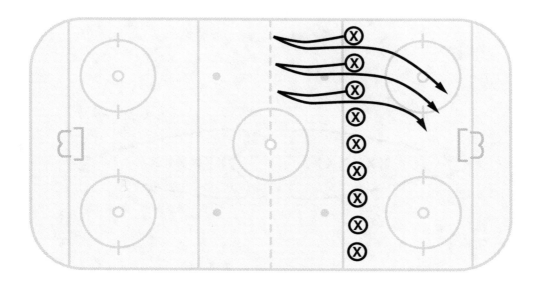

DESCRIPTION OF DRILL:
• Work both blue lines at the same time, both ends of the ice.
• Align shooters as shown and have a goaltender in the net.
• The shooters breaks for the red line, abruptly stops, crosses over to
  return into the zone for a shot on goal.
• The goalie comes out, with proper form, to meet each shooter.

COACHING POINTS:
Some coaches suggest that slapshots NOT be used in warm-ups since
there is an injury factor; this is especially important in a pregame drill.

NAME OF DRILL: Peel and Shoot Drill
SKILL TO BE TAUGHT/ENHANCED: Shooting

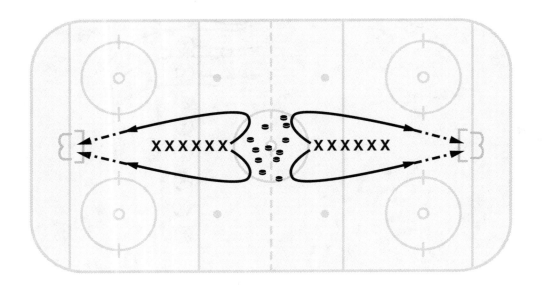

DESCRIPTION OF DRILL:
- Place the pucks at center ice and align the players in two lines as shown.
- On the whistle, the lead player on each line will peel off, pick up a loose puck and carry in for a shot on goal. Repeat with the second player going to the other side, etc.

NAME OF DRILL: Circle In and Backhand Drill
SKILL TO BE TAUGHT/ENHANCED: Puck Control, Backhand-shots

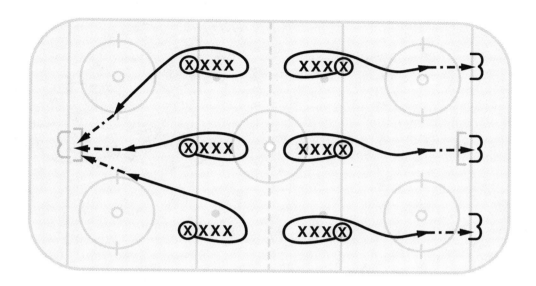

DESCRIPTION OF DRILL:
- Align three nets along the goal line and three lines of players to work against them.
- On the whistle, the lead player, with a puck, will circle his/her own line as shown. Emphasize acceleration on the turn.
- Attack the net drawing the puck to the backhand side. Shoot.
- Repeat the drill by having the players circle their lines around the other side, too.
- If you do not have enough nets, simply place a cone or chair on the ice as a target. Try to get the shooters to lift the puck.

COACHING POINTS:
In teaching the backhand to younger players, impart to them the idea that the farther away from the net they are, then the further down on the stick shaft the lower hand should be. Also, more weight transfer from back leg to front leg be needed, too. Emphasize follow-through also.

135

NAME OF DRILL: Three -Shot Drill I
SKILL TO BE TAUGHT/ENHANCED: Shooting Skills

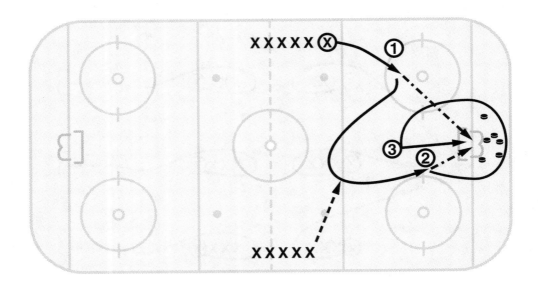

DESCRIPTION OF DRILL:
- Players are aligned in neutral zone as shown. They will alternate sides and change lines during the course of the drill.
- Three distinct shots are to be taken in this drill. #1 is a slapshot on the fly while #2 is a snapshot and #3 is a wrist shot.
- The drill opens with one player breaking in and taking the slapshot. He/she then loops back out of the zone, receives a pass from the other line and skates in for a snapper. After the shot, the shooter circles around the net, pickes up a loose puck and comes out in front for a wrist shot. You may wish to vary this shot #3 and have the player loop around the net forcing him/her to take a backhand.

COACHING POINTS:
Make shot #3 an "intellegent shot." Place a coach at the end of the line the player will be returning to and ask them to tell you where they were trying to place the puck and why. Have them conscious of the five "holes" every goalie has.

NAME OF DRILL: Three-Shot Drill II
SKILL TO BE TAUGHT/ENHANCED: Shooting

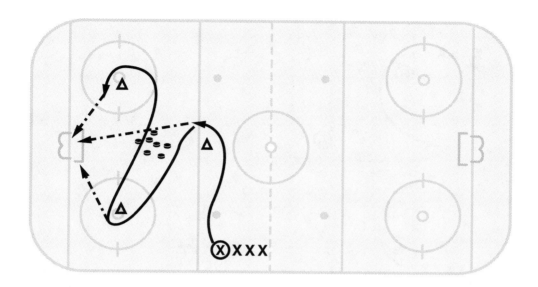

DESCRIPTION OF DRILL:
• Use both ends of the ice simultaneously.
• The player in front of the line in the neutral zone begins with a puck (or he/she can receive one from a passing coach across the ice) and breaks for the top cone. At this point they must launch a slapshot or hard snapshot/wristshot on goal. Many times they will have to shoot on the fly or pivot to get into position for a good shot.
• The player then picks up a loose puck in the slot, breaks left around the next cone to release either a snapshot or backhand. They then loop back through the slot to pick up another puck and launch yet a third shot on goal, this one also being either a snapshot or backhand. Note that one of the two lower shots MUST be a backhand.

COACHING POINTS:
Note that your players executing this drill will employ three different shots: slapper, snapshot and backhand. Emphasize this.

NAME OF DRILL: Three-Shot Drill III
SKILL TO BE TAUGHT/ENHANCED: Rapid Fire for Goalies; Slap, Wrist
(Snap) and Backhand Shots for Skaters

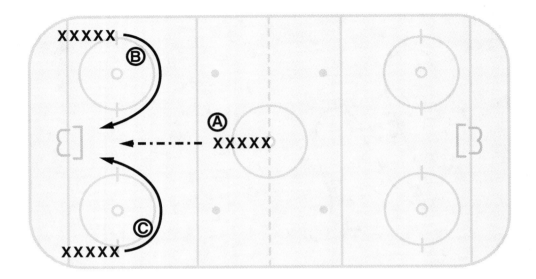

DESCRIPTION OF DRILL:
• Begin drill sequence with slap shot from line A.
• Line B and then line C follows in with either forehand or backhand
  shot depending, of course, on stick side.
• Snap shot can be emphasized over wrist shot if so desired.
• Timing can be sped up to drill goalie reactions.

COACHING POINTS:
Work your goalies, too. Have them toss their sticks aside and use only
gloves or pads or skates for reactions. Have the shooters aim for certain
locations against the goalies such as high glove side or lower left corner,
etc.

NAME OF DRILL: Three-Shot Drill IV
SKILL TO BE TAUGHT/ENHANCED: Quick Release of Shot

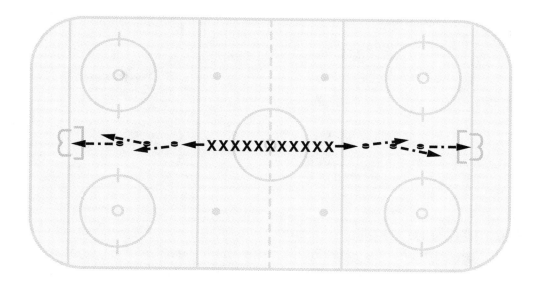

DESCRIPTION OF DRILL:
- Line your players up in the neutral zone as shown (or, if need dictates, you can set two or even three such lines). Set three pucks about five feet apart on line with the net.
- On command, a player breaks toward the goal and snaps off three quick shots using the pucks lined up for this purpose. Use the snap or wrist shot; they will not have time for the slapshot. All of the shots are to be released "on the fly."

COACHING POINTS:
Studies have shown that besides accuracy, the second most important factor in goal scoring is release time. Strive for shot release time under one second per shot.

NAME OF DRILL: Tire Drill
SKILL TO BE TAUGHT/ENHANCED: Shooting Through a Screen

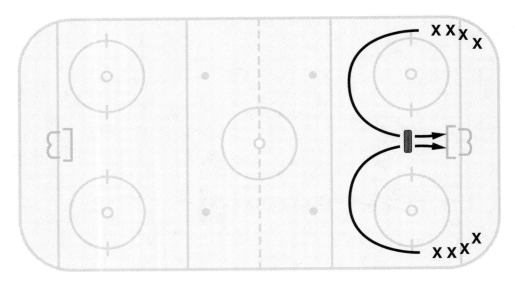

DESCRIPTION OF DRILL:
- A coaching tool needs to be made: take an old tire and nail, or otherwise attach, the tire to a piece of wood which, serving as a base, will hold the tire upright.

- Players will circle in, approach tire, and shoot on goal through the tire. Backhand and forehand should be utilized.
- Change sides after the shot.

COACHING POINTS:
- Shooters: head up, quick-release shot (i.e., wrist or snap)
- For intensified goalie work, place tire at hashmarks and have a player stand on each side of tire (they may work on tip-ins of errant shots going wide of the tire). This will build a more obscuring screen through which the goalies must find the puck and react.

NAME OF DRILL: 4-Station Shooting
SKILL TO BE TAUGHT/ENHANCED: Skating, Shooting, Attacking Net

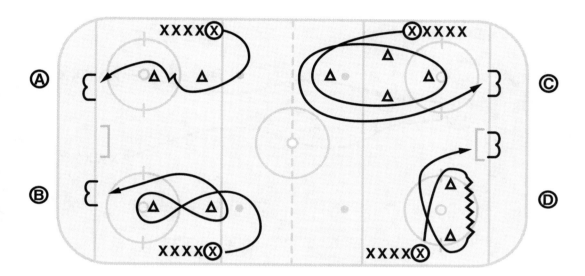

DESCRIPTION OF DRILL:
All four drills shown above entail speed skating, turns, and dekes.
DRILL A:
Deke the cone so that you attack the net on the backhand side.
DRILL B:
Figure 8 and attack.
DRILL C:
Circle in and shoot; perhaps call for a slapshot or snapshot on the fly.
DRILL D:
Break around the inner cone, pivot into a full-speed backskate, still controlling the puck, to the outer cone, pivot again and accelerate to the net.

NAME OF DRILL: Long Shot/Short Shot Drill
SKILL TO BE TAUGHT/ENHANCED: Shooting, Goalie Work

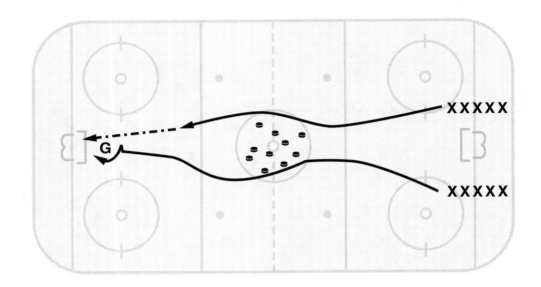

DESCRIPTION OF DRILL:
- Line the players up alongside the goalposts of one goal at one end of the ice.
- On the whistle, two players break for center ice where they each pick up a loose puck.
- The first player to reach the blue line fires a slapshot or snapshot on goal from the blue line. The second player will carry in for a deke on the goalie.
- Emphasize goalie recovery.

NAME OF DRILL: Breakaway Contest
SKILL TO BE TAUGHT/ENHANCED: Dekes, Shots, Alone on Goalie

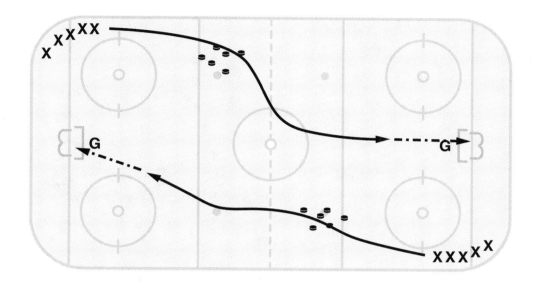

DESCRIPTION OF DRILL:
• Align players in opposite and diagonal corners; place pucks near offside
  faceoff dots.
• Alternating, players go in on goaltenders for simulated breakaway.
• For an added element of fun with advanced players, have them show
  off their best move/deke. Call it the Hot Dog Drill. (This drill can also
  be done against a shooting board.)

COACHING POINTS:
• Work on goalies coming out, backskating in and forcing the shooter to
  make the first move.
• Have the players work on their "breakaway read:" if goalie is out, deke;
  if goalie is deep in net, shoot.
• Coaches are advised to keep a close eye on who wins this drill on a
  consistent basis since you may find yourself in a shoot-out tie-breaker
  and the players who win this drill in practice may help you win a
  game. They may not always be your top scorer in regular game situations.

NAME OF DRILL: Tip-In Drill
SKILL TO BE TAUGHT/ENHANCED: Offensive Tip-ins and Screens

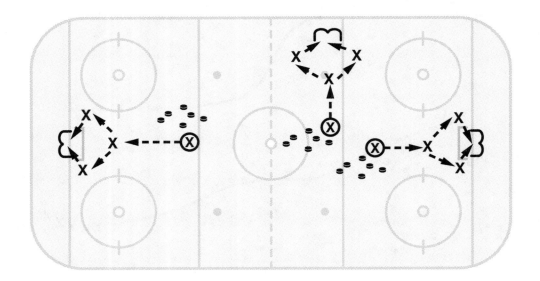

DESCRIPTION OF DRILL:
- Nets can be placed anywhere along the boards; teams of four players should be used and goalies may or may not be present.
- The shooter places himself with a pile of pucks about 20 feet from the net and fires low, hard snapshots at the posts. The players along the side of the crease are to tip the pucks in; the middle player can act as a screen or work on defecting and re-directing straight-on shots.

COACHING POINTS:
Wingers should come away with a sense of emphasis on what I preach to my players as "post-control." We need to have our wings drive to the posts in the offensive zone, especially the wing away from the puck.

NAME OF DRILL: Deflection Drill
SKILL TO BE TAUGHT/ENHANCED: Tin-ins, Re-directions, Deflections

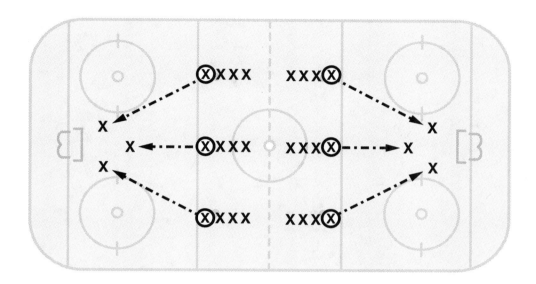

DESCRIPTION OF DRILL:
- Shooters (or coaches) align at blue line, three across.
- Deflecters align in a triangulation near the nets as shown.
- Shooter must keep the shot hard and on the ice (or no more than 6" off it).
- Deflecters must get a stick on the puck somehow. Emphasize that they must keep their sticks on the ice.
- Shoot on the whistle rather than all at once.

NAME OF DRILL: Fallen Goalie Drill
SKILL TO BE TAUGHT/ENHANCED: Close-in Goal line Scramble Shots
vs. a Goalie Lying on the Ice

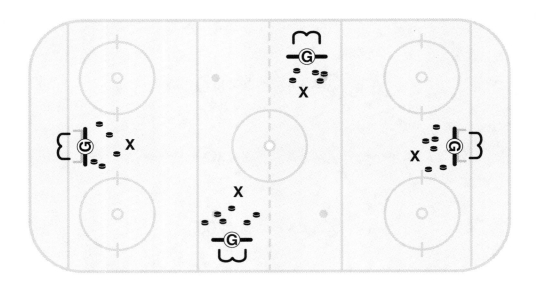

DESCRIPTION OF DRILL:
- Set as many nets and goalies around the ice as is possible. Technically, a net is not needed if more goalies than nets are available. If there are more nets than goalies, use regular players.
- Place the goalies in a stack-pad save position lying on the ice.
- Lay pucks just outside the goalie and goalmouth, perhaps 12" to 18" away.
- The shooter must flip the puck, with quick hand action and a "scooping" technique with the open-face of the stickblade, over the fallen goalie. Some shooters may prefer to draw the puck back first, but time does not often permit this technique when there is a scramble of players being checked in front.

COACHING POINTS:
Goalies can benefit from this drill, too. They must use their glove/blocker hand and/or "scissor" the legpads to stop the shot.

NAME OF DRILL: Double-Deke Shooting Drill
SKILL TO BE TAUGHT/ENHANCED: Puckhandling, Offensive Skills

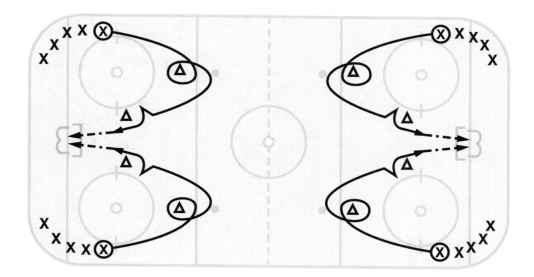

DESCRIPTION OF DRILL:
- Align players in the corners and place cones near the blue line and hashmark.
- On the whistle, the player will break for the cone, execute a tight hockey turn around the cone, deke the second cone and then shoot.
- Have them switch lines after the shot.

NAME OF DRILL: Circle In/Two-Shot Drill
SKILL TO BE TAUGHT/ENHANCED: Skating, Pass Receiving, Shooting

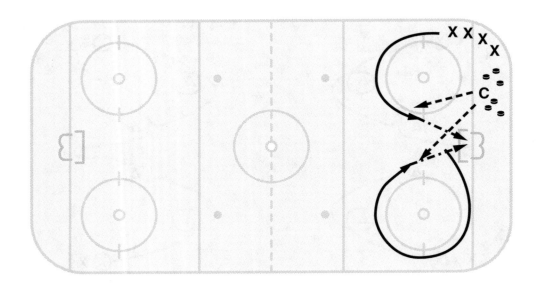

DESCRIPTION OF DRILL:
- Players align in corner as shown. Coach stands, with pucks, beside the net.
- Player breaks around faceoff circle emphasizing acceleration.
- Player receives the pass and quickly releases the shot; he or she will then break around the other circle, skating and crossing over in the other direction, only to return to the slot for another shot.
- The drill can be replicated on the other half of the ice surface.

COACHING POINTS:
- Have players work on one-timing their shot or, at the very least, work on getting their shot off in under one second!
- Players should accelerate on their crossovers "running on their toes." Make this a hi-tempo drill for your more advanced skaters.

NAME OF DRILL: Rebound Drill
SKILL TO BE TAUGHT/ENHANCED: Attacking the net and seeking rebounds, Following up the shot

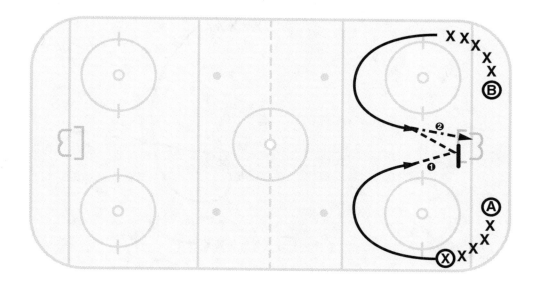

DESCRIPTION OF DRILL:
- Several devices can be used to facilitate this drill. You may wish to bring your "fallen goalie" board in from the outside off-ice shooting area or you may wish to use a canvas net cover ("Shooter Tutor").
- Line the players up as shown. Players in line A will preceed those in Line B into the zone, take a shot, and since the board allows a rebound, the players in line B will follow it up, shooting the rebound into the net.
- Be sure to station a coach by the net to pass a puck out to the follow-up player if no rebound is created (i.e., the first shot went either into the net or wide).
- You may wish to use live goalies and a coach to pass out pucks because the rebounds are less predictable in this case.

COACHING POINTS:
This drill can also be done with only one player line. Have them take the initial shot out by the blue-line and then break for their own rebound, either a created one or a pass-out by the coach.

149

NAME OF DRILL: Re-Acceleration Shooting Drill
SKILL TO BE TAUGHT/ENHANCED: Quick Acceleration with Puck

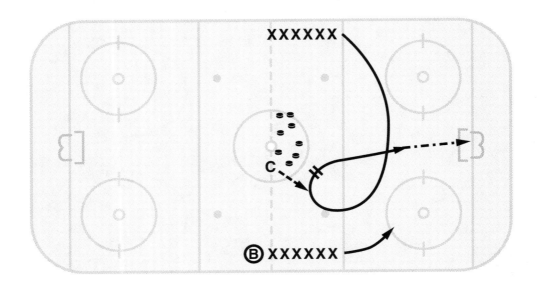

DESCRIPTION OF DRILL:
- There are two phases to this shooting drill.
- The players are to be aligned in groups along the neutral zone boards as shown. The coach is in the center-ice faceoff circle and he/she has the pucks.
- On command a player from one side breaks into the zone, across the top of the circles, back across the line into the neutral zone where they will receive a pass from the coach. They then STOP.
- The player must then re-accelerate, with quick feet, back into an attack mode. Repeat with other line mirroring the drill.
- If you wish to incorporate a phase II to this drill, have the player, from Line B shown above replicate the skating pattern, but serve as a checker.

COACHING POINTS:
Use both ends of the ice simultaneously.

NAME OF DRILL: 8-in-Front Quick-Shot Drill
SKILL TO BE TAUGHT/ENHANCED: Shooting, Shot Release Time

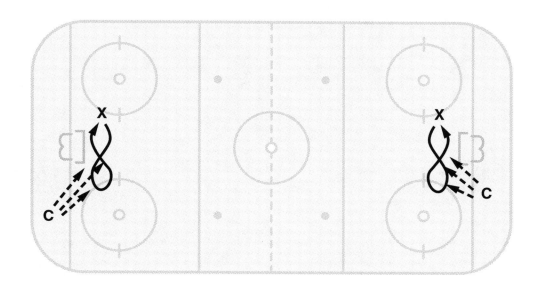

DESCRIPTION OF DRILL:
• The player in front of the net skates a hard, quick figure-8, always with his/her stick on the ice. The coach behind will pass pucks out and the shooter must quickly release forehand snapshots or backhands on net.
• There is no opponent defending the slot in this drill.

COACHING POINTS:
Emphasize keeping the stick on the ice and getting the shot away quickly.

NAME OF DRILL: Post/Shooter Drill
SKILL TO BE TAUGHT/ENHANCED: Post Coverage, both from Shooter and Goalies' Perspectives

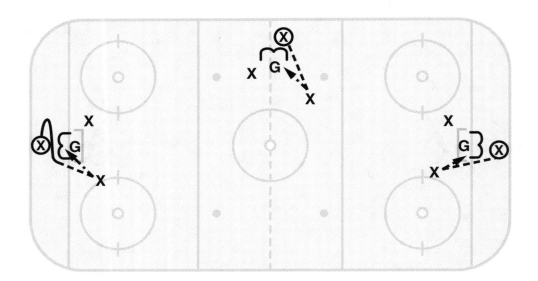

DESCRIPTION OF DRILL:
- Place a shooter at edge of crease and near each post. Place a passer from behind the net into position behind goal.
- Passer will work puck out to one of the shooters who will be expected to one-time the shot.
- Goalie must work his/her slide-n-glide post coverage as well as anticipation skills.

COACHING POINTS:
If you have several nets and goalies available, why not place several around the rink? This drill works with three shooters and one goalie. Try to get a lot of people involved.

NAME OF DRILL: Goal Line Drill
SKILL TO BE TAUGHT/ENHANCED: Quickness to Net, Goalie Reaction
and Post-to-Post Movement

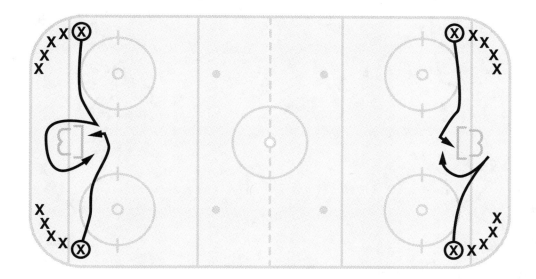

DESCRIPTION OF DRILL:
- Skater: cut straight toward net along the goalline and then they read
  goalie on post coverage; they have option of carrying behind net for a
  wrap-around or driving into slot.
- Goalie must react to skater and cover post-to-post. Skater can be cre-
  ative in this drill: fake wrap-around and return to near post; fake backhand in front and pull back forehand shot in front, etc.

NAME OF DRILL: Deep-in-the-Slot-Shot Drill
SKILL TO BE TAUGHT/ENHANCED: Shooting in Close to Net

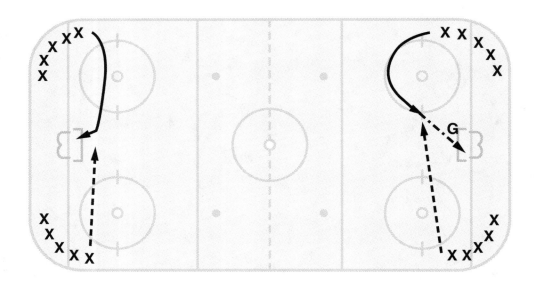

DESCRIPTION OF DRILL:
- Use both ends at once and align the players in the corners as shown.
- Have a goalie in one net and leave the other net open.
- Drill A has no goalie, but B does. In either case the shooter must receive a pass from the other corner and, while remaining shallow to the goalline, one-time a shot home. The players in Drill B, who face a goalie, are allowed to go out a bit further, but no deeper than the faceoff dots.
- After the passer releases, they then skate to the net as a shooter; switch lines after shooting.

COACHING POINTS:
Don't actually "shoot" the hard cross-crease pass; simply angle the stick on the ice to deflect it toward the center of the net. (If you angle the deflection for a corner, oftentimes the force of the pass will cause the stick to deflect the puck wide.)

NAME OF DRILL: Dot-Slot-Post Drill
SKILL TO BE TAUGHT/ENHANCED: Shooting

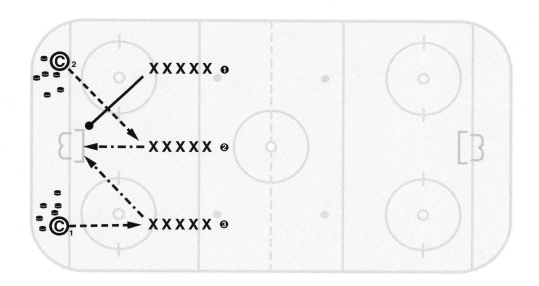

DESCRIPTION OF DRILL:
- This drill can be run at both ends of the ice simultaneously. Goalies may or may not be involved.
- Set two coaches, with pucks, in the corners (they can be replaced by proficient players). There will be a line of shooters set up at each endzone faceoff dot and in the high slot (i.e., no lower than the hashmarks).
- Coach #1 will pass off to Line #3 first and a shot will be taken, preferably a one-timer. As this pass is launched, the skater in Line #1 will break for their near post seeking a tip-in or rebound. They will remain there for the shot taken by both Line #1 and Line #2.
- After the shot is taken by Line #3, Coach #2 passes into the slot to a forward in Line #2; he/she also shoots.

COACHING POINTS:
- Make sure that all forwards keep their sticks on the ice with stiff lower-hand pressure. Also see to it that they are in position for the shot prior to receiving the pass.
- Reverse the lines after each round of shooting.
- If goalies are involved, have them working on shuffle-glide and stuffing the rebound off the post.

NAME OF DRILL: Golden Arches Attack Drill
SKILL TO BE TAUGHT/ENHANCED: Passing, Shooting

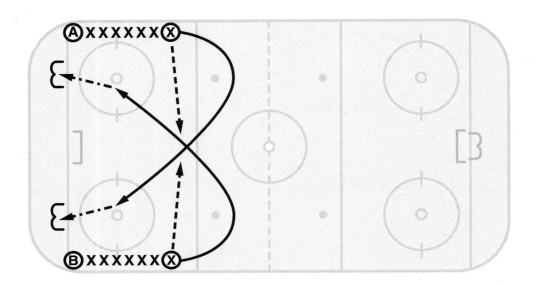

DESCRIPTION OF DRILL:
- Align players along boards as shown. Use both ends of the ice simultaneously. Note the use of two nets in each zone.
- Players from Line A will circle in and receive pass from players in Line B. Upon launching the pass, that player should break to receive a pass from their opposite line.
- This drill can also be used as a pre-game warm-up, although only one net would be used then.

NAME OF DRILL: Loop-Pass-Shoot-Rebound Drill
SKILL TO BE TAUGHT/ENHANCED: Offensive Skills

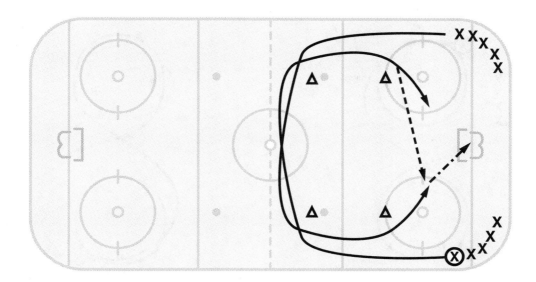

DESCRIPTION OF DRILL:
- Players align in corners as shown. On the whistle the lead player in each line breaks around the neutral zone cones as shown; one has a puck.
- Note they must each skate hard around the perimeter of the cones.
- Once clearing their designated cone, the puck carrying skater passes off to his/her partner who, in turn, shoots on goal while the other player reads and breaks for the rebound.
- A drop-pass pattern may also be called for by the coach; similarly the coach may call for two touch-passes before the shot.

NAME OF DRILL: 8-In and Shoot Drill
SKILL TO BE TAUGHT/ENHANCED: Skating with Pucks, Shooting

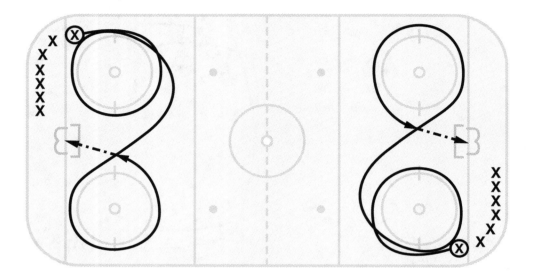

DESCRIPTION OF DRILL:
- Line the players in each corner with pucks; on the whistle, the lead skater in each line will aggressively attack each circle in a figure-8 pattern, accelerating along the way.
- They finish with a shot on goal.
- Use both ends of the ice simultaneously. Work the drill from the direction upon completion to one side.

NAME OF DRILL: The Shooting Arc Drill
SKILL TO BE TAUGHT/ENHANCED: Shooting, Quick Release, Pivots
and Squaring up to the Shot

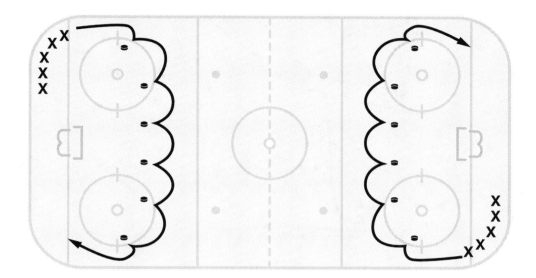

DESCRIPTION OF DRILL:
- Line the players up in the corners as shown and place an arc of pucks across the perimeter of the faceoff circles and hi-slot as drawn.
- Using both ends of the ice and one player at a time, the lead player on each line, at the whistle, is to skate the arc shooting each puck with the forehand or backhand as his/her stick positioning dictates.
- Emphasize quick release, constant movement, good shoulder positioning and not "walking around the backhand."
- Upon completion of the arc, have the player line up in the far corner and return along the arc for work with his/her "other" hand, i.e., forehand or backhand.

COACHING POINTS:
Coaches may wish to emphasize wrist or snapshot on the forehand, so call it out at the beginning of the drill.

NAME OF DRILL: BU Two-Shot Drill
SKILL TO BE TAUGHT/ENHANCED: Shooting, Passing, Give-n-Go Skills

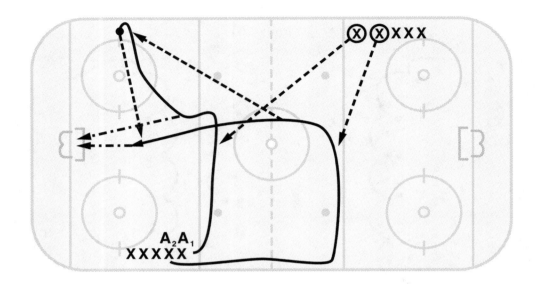

DESCRIPTION OF DRILL:
• Line players along boards near the neutral zone as shown.
• On the whistle, the front two players in line A will break along the blue lines designated in the diagram, one going deep and the other near. Both will receive a pass from their respective front two players in Line B.
• Player A1 will shoot at the blue line/hi-slot area and proceed into the offensive zone, setting up along the boards at the hashmarks.
• Player A2, coming through the neutral zone with the puck received from the second player in Line B, will execute a give-n-go with player A1 taking his shot from the slot.
• After passing off in the give-n-go, player A1 should break for the net looking for the rebound.
• Then have Line B replicate the drill at their end of the ice.

(Credit for this drill should go to USA Hockey's fine publication, "American Hockey" in which they run a drill-of-the-month feature. For drill fanatics like myself, this is an eagerly awaited column.)

NAME OF DRILL: Corner Turn-N-Shoot Drill
SKILL TO BE TAUGHT/ENHANCED: Advanced Offensive Skills

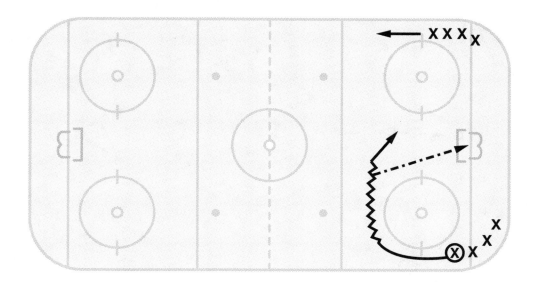

DESCRIPTION OF DRILL:
- Line players in the corners. Upon the whistle, the lead player breaks to the top of the faceoff circle carrying the puck, pivots into a backskate mode and fires the puck, while moving across the top of the circle and into the slot. Emphasize the snap shot.
- Repeat with the other line and alternate sides.
- Have the players change sides after each shot.
- Use both ends of the ice simultaneously.

161

NAME OF DRILL: 2-0 Crash-The-Net Drill
SKILL TO BE TAUGHT/ENHANCED: Rebound Shots, Goalies' Control of Rebounds

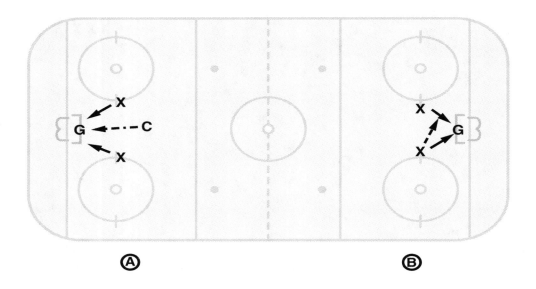

Ⓐ   Ⓑ

DESCRIPTION OF DRILL:
- There are two ways to run this drill and both are diagrammed. Drill A employs a coach to shoot a puck into the goalie's pads to create rebound while Drill B simply has one of two players do this.
- In either case, players scramble for the rebound, as does the goalie. This creates a "desperation mentality." Once the rebound is taken in by the netminder, he/she must release it out toward the hashmarks within two seconds to continue the drill.
- The drill ends when the offense scores or when the puck trickles past the goalline.

COACHING POINTS:
Time the players and make this drill competitive.

NAME OF DRILL: Dot Shots Drill
SKILL TO BE TAUGHT/ENHANCED: Power Play, Coordination Between Points/Wings

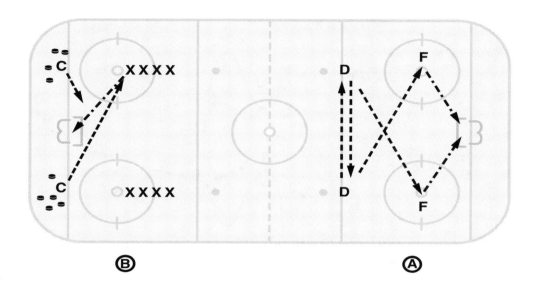

DESCRIPTION OF DRILL:
- Set two defensemen at the points and two forwards on the endzone dots. On the whistle, the two pointmen will pass between themselves for a predetermined number of passes. Then they will pass the puck across the attacking zone to the winger or forward set up for a one-time shot on the dots. (A)
- A good variation of this drill is to have coaches pass the puck out from the side of the net below the goalline. They will pass diagonally out to a waiting forward on the dots, similar to the drill shown above. (B)
- Also, work your goalies in their nets with "post-to-post" set-ups.

COACHING POINTS:
Teach proper set-up for the one-timed shot. Although opinions vary, I like to have the shooter line up his or her outside shoulder (away from the passer) on the nearside post. This accomodates the "open to the net" or "open to the passer" techniques emphasized by various coaches. The weight should be on the back foot and the stick poised in a shooting position. The shooter is taught to "drive through the puck."

NAME OF DRILL: Cut-Weave-and-Stay Onside!
SKILL TO BE TAUGHT/ENHANCED: Tactical Position Play, Shooting

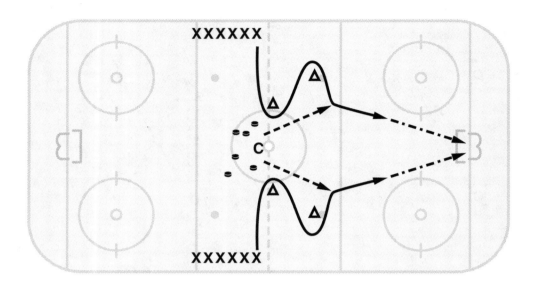

DESCRIPTION OF DRILL:
- Line the players along the boards in the neutral zone and set a coach with pucks in the center-ice faceoff circle. Set cones near the perimeter of the circle and on the faceoffs dots.
- On a whistle, one player will weave through the cones at top speed, simulating the notion of "getting open" for the pass. Rounding the second cone, he/she must stay onside until the coach hits them with a pass. They may then cut in for the shot on goal.
- Alternate sides on command.
- Use both ends of the ice simultaneously.

NAME OF DRILL: Long Shot/Tip-In Drill
SKILL TO BE TAUGHT/ENHANCED: Shooting, Deflections

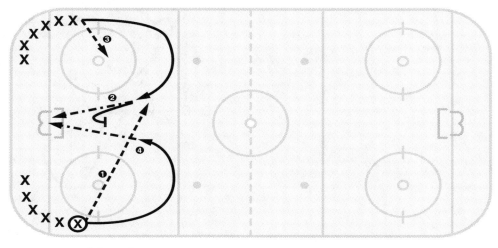

Line A

DESCRIPTION OF DRILL:
• Use both ends of the ice at once, setting players in each of the corners. All lines need pucks.
• Two passes and two shots will be taken.
• On the whistle, the lead player breaks to the blue line and receives a pass from the opposite line. He/she is to shoot at once and break to the front of the cage to set a screen in front of the netminder.
• After the passer who launched pass #1 has released the puck for the pass, they are to replicate the drill by breaking for the blue line, receiving the pass, shooting and then setting their own screen.
• In reading this diagram, #1 is a pass, #2 is a long shot, #3 a pass and #4 a shot.

COACHING POINTS:
Players must keep the long shots low and hard, no more than six inches off the ice.

NAME OF DRILL: Double Screen Tip-In Drill
SKILL TO BE TAUGHT/ENHANCED: Screens, Tip-ins, Passing

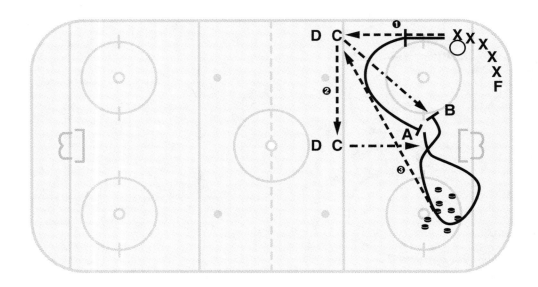

DESCRIPTION OF DRILL:
- Use both ends of the ice simultaneously, but only one half is diagrammed here for the sake of clarity. This drill is not as complex as it first appears.
- Forwards are aligned in one corner and defensemen or coaches will play the points.
- On the whistle the lead forward launched pass #1 to the near pointman who, in turn, passes across to the other point. The latter will shoot on goal. In the meantime, the forward who first passed has looped around the top of the near circle and positioned himself for a screen (A).
- After tipping/deflecting the first shot, he/she breaks into the other circle for a loose puck which is passed across the zone to the far point. That pointman will shoot and the forward has by then positioned himself for a second screen (B).

COACHING POINTS:
Although your defensemen may be getting work on their point play, you may wish to use the other end of the ice for another facet of their game — clearing passes. Rob Abel, assistant coach at Dartmouth told me that he actually tapes an "X" on the glass for clearing passes and has his defensemen aim at these points.

FUN 'N' GAMES

–Games for younger players

–"Small ice" games for advanced players

"Hard work is relative to what you're used to."

Coach Dick Vermiel

NAME OF DRILL: Seek-and-Find Drill
SKILL TO BE TAUGHT/ENHANCED: Passing, Reading Openings, Keeping Head Up

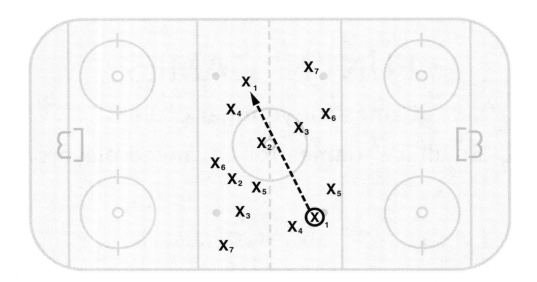

DESCRIPTION OF DRILL:
- Each player is assigned a partner and all sets of partners are told to station themselves in a designated portion of the ice.
- On the whistle, all of the players begin moving within the confines of their ice section.
- Since only one of the two partners has a puck, they must find their mate and pass the puck to them when they are open. (For the sake of diagram clarity, I have not shown the players as moving, but realize that they will once the drill begins.) Use two pucks at once. Partners without pucks must intercept and when they do, they must seek out their partner to pass to.

COACHING POINTS:
- Teach players to "read openings" and jump into them for a pass.
- In the diagram shown above, there are 14 players (7 tandems). This number would be for smaller players; the larger your players the more room you will need, so cut down on the number of partners but still keep in mind that the philosophy of the drill is to create "traffic."

NAME OF DRILL: Relay Races
SKILL TO BE TAUGHT/ENHANCED: Skating Speed, Team Competitiveness

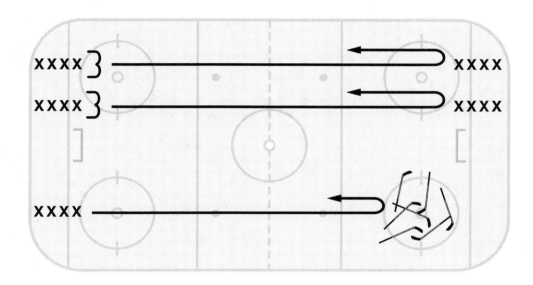

DESCRIPTION OF DRILL:
There are many variations that coaches can work in relay races. Here are some that may be incorporated:
NET PUSH
Team A-1 pushes net down to Team A-2, then A-2 returns net to position from which A-1 began. In the meantime, A-1 has returned to position. Can repeat several times. Use 1-3 players.
BRING HOME THE BACON
A more traditional relay race, this one calls for players to lay their sticks in far endzone corner circle. Race from one circle, retrieve stick and return to "home" circle.
VARIATIONS (not shown)
For generally older players, have then perform "suicides" between blue lines, fore- and backskating, weave through cones, etc., but in relay race format.

COACHING POINTS:
In each relay race, there are, of course two, three, four or even five teams.

NAME OF DRILL: Shooting Arcade Drill
SKILL TO BE TAUGHT/ENHANCED: Shooting, Passing Accuracy

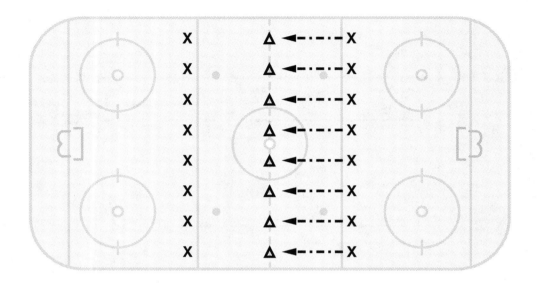

DESCRIPTION OF DRILL:
- Largely for younger players, this is a fun drill to end practice.
- Line players along blue lines as shown. One side shoots at a time and their targets are cones, the lighter the better.
- On the whistle, blast 'em off the red line! Winners leave the ice or win a soda or whatever....
- For a lesson in humility, let the coaches shoot, too.

NAME OF DRILL: Murder Ball
SKILL TO BE TAUGHT/ENHANCED: Skating Balance, Agility
DURATION OF DRILL: 5 min.

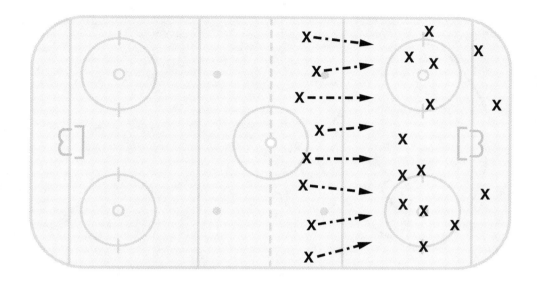

DESCRIPTION OF DRILL:
• Choose two teams (base them on helmet or jersey color for ease and quickness).
• One team is in neutral zone with either tennis balls or all-purpose rubber balls; they will try to hit other team, scattered about and skating in one of the deep ends.
• If hit, player is out; if he/she catches thrown ball, then the thrower is out.
• No one is allowed to skate beyond opponents' blue line and team being thrown at can counter-attack at random with the same rules applying.

COACHING POINTS:
• Begin the game by dumping balls in center-ice faceoff circle with both teams on their respective blue lines.
• This drill is a rendition of the old gym-class standard, a.k.a. "bombardment."
• If drill begins to lag, allow bounced/rebounding balls to count as "hits."

171

NAME OF DRILL: 5-on-5 Puckball
SKILL TO BE TAUGHT/ENHANCED: Skating Speed, Turns, Passing

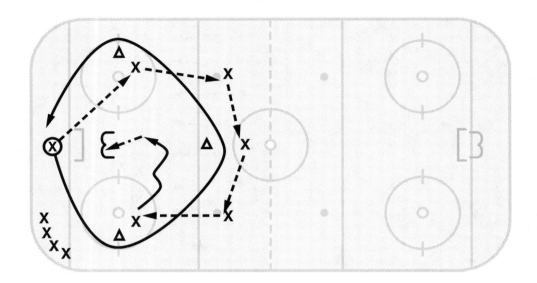

DESCRIPTION OF DRILL:
- Two games will be going on simultaneously, each is one-half of the ice.
- Move nets up to hash marks.
- Set five players out "in the field" as shown by those circled.
- Set teams "at bat" in corner and have one "batter" step forward to crease where he/she then flips, passes, lofts, or shoots puck into an open area. (Puck must stay inside rink and it must not cross the red line or it is an "out.")
- Players in field must retrieve puck and then receive pass from each player before shooting it into net. If shooters score before "batter" races around bases, it is an out. If "batter" makes it around bases first (note cones) then the offensive team gets a run. Play three outs.

COACHING POINTS:
Keep the game moving as there can be substantial "standing around" if not.

NAME OF DRILL: Soccer Hockey
SKILL TO BE TAUGHT/ENHANCED: Skating Balance, Agility
DURATION OF DRILL: 7-10 min.

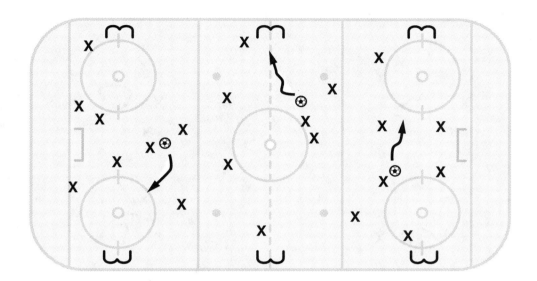

DESCRIPTION OF DRILL:
• Depending upon the number of players you have, set up one, two, or three cross-ice or full-ice soccer games to be played on skates. Use real soccer balls (often the more "dead" the ball, the better the game) and you will be amazed at the way the kids, particularly the younger ones, attack this game.
• This drill is simply one of the finest for developing balance and agility in developmental players.

COACHING POINTS:
Larionov's Variation: The Russian great Igor Larionov, upon reporting to the Detroit Red Wings after a trade, brought a soccer ball on to the ice and had his new teammates play this game, too. His variation, however, was the rule/objective that the ball never be allowed to touch the ice!

NAME OF DRILL: Bull In The Ring
SKILL TO BE TAUGHT/ENHANCED: Balance, Being "Tough on Skates"

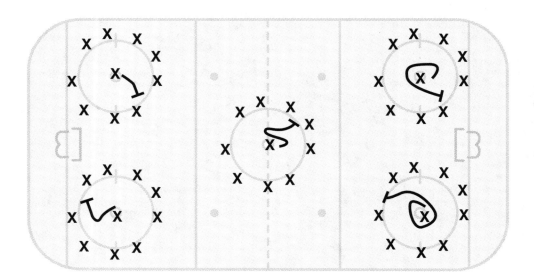

DESCRIPTION OF DRILL:
- Primarily for younger players, set them up in all five faceoff circles. No one has a hockey stick.
- Put one player in the middle.
- On the whistle he or she must pick out one player and get by/through/over them to escape. If they succeed, then the player who let them out is now in the middle.

COACHING POINTS:
Teach getting low and pushing off inside edges of skates.

NAME OF DRILL: Game — "Freeze Tag"
SKILL TO BE TAUGHT/ENHANCED: Skating, Agility
DURATION OF DRILL: 3-5 min.

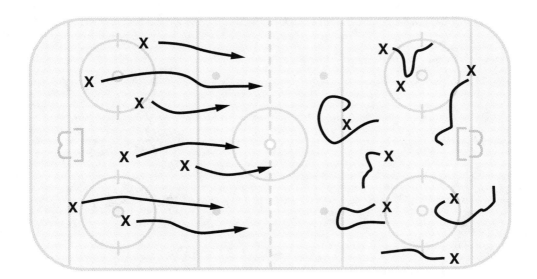

DESCRIPTION OF DRILL:
• Set up two teams of players (coaches can play, too!).
• One team is "it" while other must evade their tag.
• When tagged, a player must drop to one knee and raise hand to indi-
  cate that he/she needs to be freed up. Any player can free up another
  player as long as they are not on team that is "it." Switch teams when
  through.
• Begin in zones as shown, but allow full ice after opening whistle.
• No sticks.

COACHING POINTS:
Good for young players ... and good for coaches who are tired and willing
to be tagged!

NAME OF DRILL: Game — Bumper Cars
SKILL TO BE TAUGHT/ENHANCED: Backskating, Balance, Hip-Check

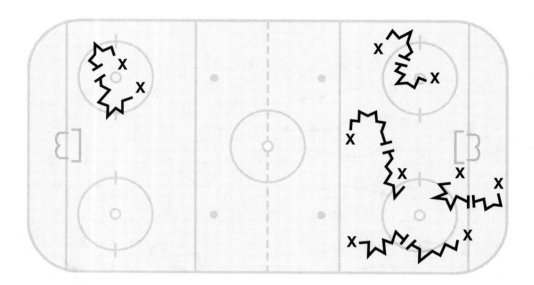

DESCRIPTION OF DRILL:
- Arrange players in enclosed areas such as a single zone or a circle. They are to foreskate at random until coach blows whistle at which time they backskate and bump into each other while backward skating.
- Be sure that they have full equipment.
- Use no sticks.

COACHING POINTS:
Younger skaters need only emphasize the backskating component, but if you wish to work this drill with older players (more skilled) then you may wish to incorporate the mechanics of swinging the hip and thrusting the leg into the hip-check.

NAME OF DRILL: E Pluribus Unum Drill
SKILL TO BE TAUGHT/ENHANCED: Stickhandling, Passing, Checking, Teamwork

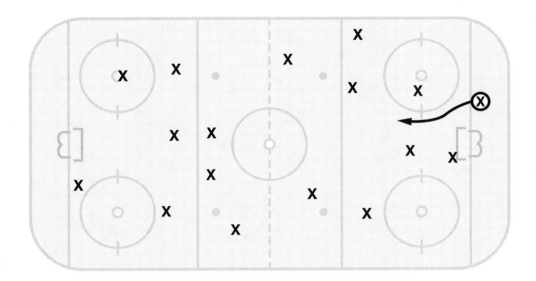

DESCRIPTION OF DRILL:
• One player has the puck and begins a rush up ice from his goalline.
• The rest of the team is scattered about in all three of the zones he will attempt to carry through. They are allowed to skate after him and check the puck away; however, they are confined to the zone they are assigned to.
• The checking team should be successful in taking the puck away from a solitary puck carrier! However, when the puck is gained, the drill starts over again with two players (the original carrier and the player who stole the puck from the original player).
• Keep adding players to the rushing team as they take the puck away. You may prefer to use several pucks or one which is passed by the "rushing" players.

COACHING POINTS:
Another variation of this game/drill, which actually takes little time at the end of practice, is to have coaches and goalies form up in the neutral zone and the rest of the team tries to make it from one end zone to the other. Any player whose stick or puck is poked, touched or checked must join the checkers (coaches and goalies).

177

NAME OF DRILL: Multi-Scrimmage
SKILL TO BE TAUGHT/ENHANCED: Scrimmaging, Heads-up Puck Control

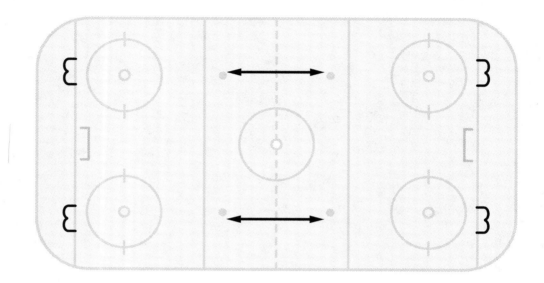

DESCRIPTION OF DRILL:
- Divide the players into four teams and place two nets on each goalline.
- The players will scrimmage for the full length of the ice, but they are roughly confined to one-half of the ice surface lengthwise.
- They may shoot only into designated nets.

NAME OF DRILL: 3-Man Puck Movement Game
SKILL TO BE TAUGHT/ENHANCED: Passing, Quick Shots, Quick Passes

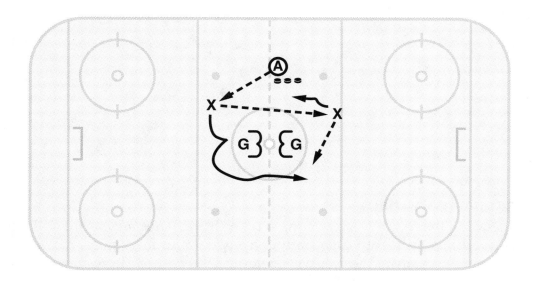

DESCRIPTION OF DRILL:
- Begin the drill with one player and three pucks stationed near the neutral zone dots as shown. The nets will be along the red line in a back-to-back formation, again, as shown. (Allow a skating lane between them, however).
- You may wish to keep the player with three pucks stationary or you can involve him/her as a skater in the game. Goalies should be in the nets.
- Player A, with three pucks, passes to one of his/her teammates to open the drill. The players must pass off to each other in such a way that all three will have touched the puck before a shot is taken.
- Once all three have touched the puck, score a goal as quickly as you can since the next puck will be sent out (or picked up loosely if you have involved Player A in the game) immediately.

COACHING POINTS:
Time this drill to make it competitive. They must score three goals in less than one minute (how about 30 seconds?!).

179

NAME OF DRILL: 3-On-3 Short Game
SKILL TO BE TAUGHT/ENHANCED: Individual Skills, 3-Man Passing, Teamwork

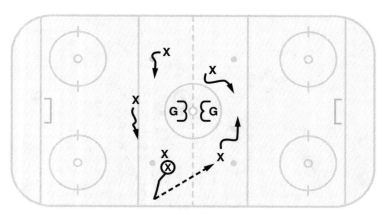

DESCRIPTION OF DRILL:
This is a close-order scrimmage to enhance not only individual stickhandling skills, but also finding an open man for a pass. All of the games are played in the neutral zone and there are three variations, hence the set of neutral zone diagrams.

DRILL A:
Play 3-on-3 with the nets facing each other along the boards.
DRILL B:
Play 3-on-3 with the nets facing each other along the blue lines.
DRILL C:
• Play 3-on-3 with the nets back-to-back along the red line (allow a skating space between them, however).
• Always use goalies.

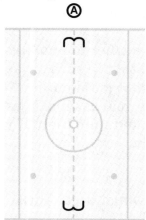

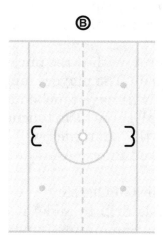

NAME OF DRILL: Two-On-Two Half-Ice
SKILL TO BE TAUGHT/ENHANCED: Scrimmaging, All Phases of Individual Skills
DURATION OF DRILL: 45-90 sec.

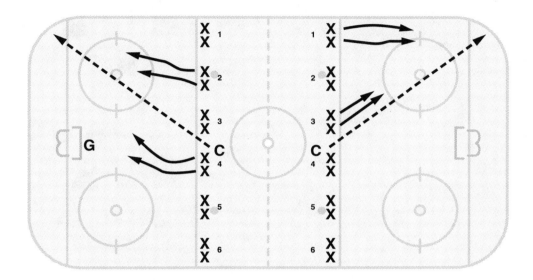

DESCRIPTION OF DRILL:
• Align your players along the blue lines in paired and numbered sets.
• Place a goalie in each net.
• Upon the commands of "1!," "2!," "3!" or "4!" those designated players will chase after a puck dumped in by the coach and proceed to scrimmage with high-speed intensity for the duration of a shift, two-on-two.
• Three-on-three can be very effective, too.

COACHING POINTS:
Younger players seem to enjoy this drill more if you assign team names such as Rangers, Devils, Black Hawks, Kings, etc. rather than numbers. They will remember their assignments better, too!

NAME OF DRILL: Small Ice 3-on-3
SKILL TO BE TAUGHT/ENHANCED: Combo Passing, Reading Teammates

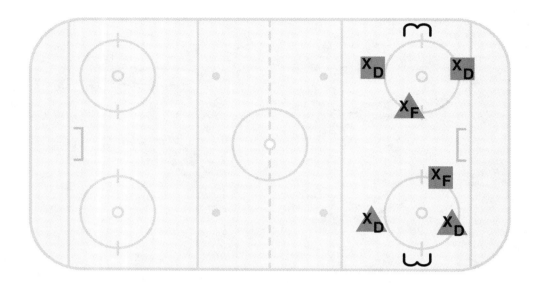

DESCRIPTION OF DRILL:

- This "small ice" game is played in one zone with three players against three (designated by teams in triangular or squared boxes).
- The defensemen initiate the play by securing the puck and they may join the rush ONLY if they complete a pass to their forward. In effect, this game creates a 1-on-2 with the potential of a 2-on-2 if the forward can break loose and receive the pass.
- Note that there is an imaginary line across the zone dividing it in half. Defencemen must remain behind that envisioned line until the pass is completed. If the other team checks their forward off the puck the defenceman must retreat.

NAME OF DRILL: Small Ice Corner Game
SKILL TO BE TAUGHT/ENHANCED: All Skills, Increase Tempo/Reaction Times

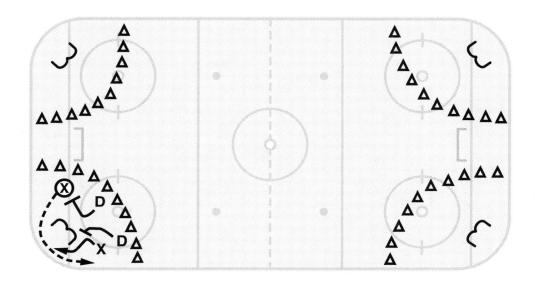

DESCRIPTION OF DRILL:
• Use all four corners for this drill if you have enough nets (you can use cones if not), but block them off with traffic cones.
• Play 2-on-2 within the closed-in space.
• Remember, small ice games increase speed, reactions and anticipation. Everything that happens in full ice games happens in small ice games, only quicker and more often.
• Note how the nets are turned to face the boards. Goalies may be used.

COACHING POINTS:
There is a passing technique which highly skilled players cultivate in which they actually pass off the net rim. This drill can develop that technique.

APPENDIX AND ACKNOWLEDGEMENTS

PRACTICE PLAN

Date: **Time:**

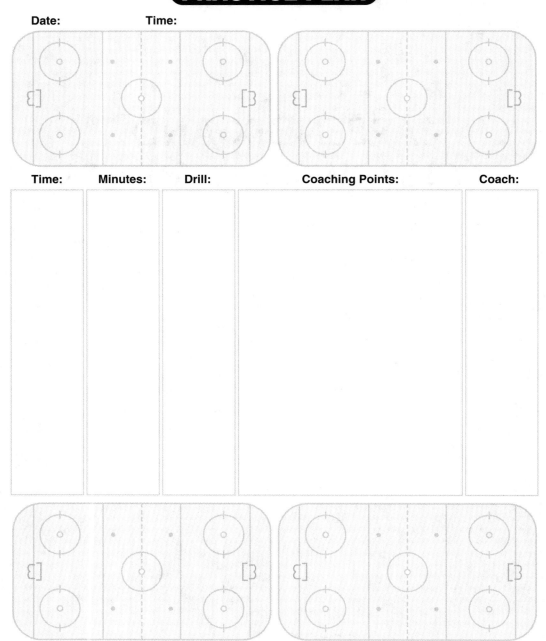

Time:	Minutes:	Drill:	Coaching Points:	Coach:

(Sample: Permission to copy granted from the author)

PRACTICE PLAN

Date: **Time:**

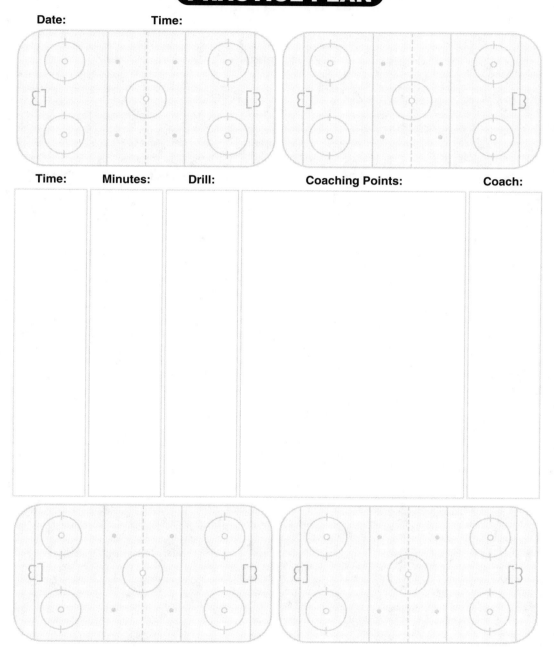

Time:	Minutes:	Drill:	Coaching Points:	Coach:

PRACTICE PLAN

Date: **Time:**

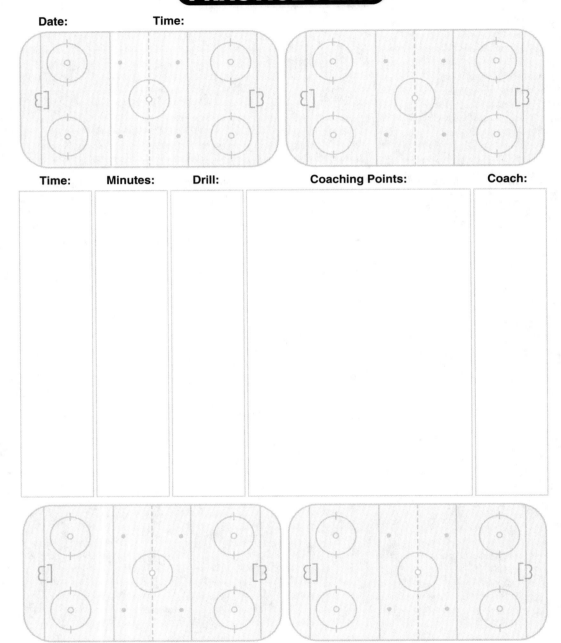

Time:	**Minutes:**	**Drill:**	**Coaching Points:**	**Coach:**

PRACTICE PLAN

Date: **Time:**

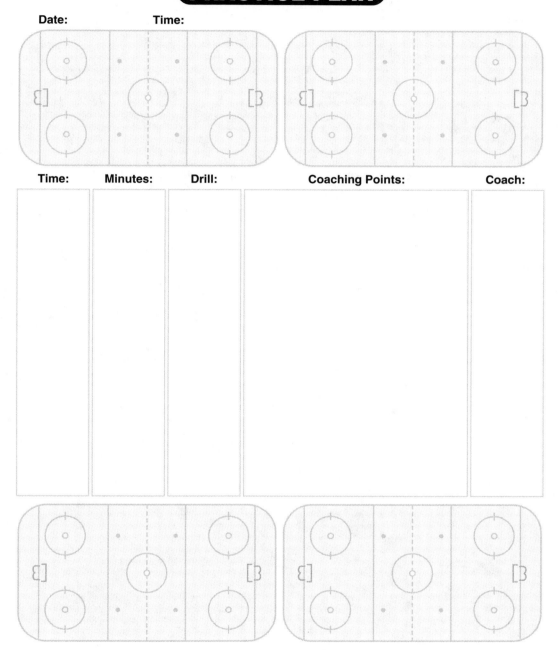

Time:	Minutes:	Drill:	Coaching Points:	Coach:

PRACTICE PLAN

Date: **Time:**

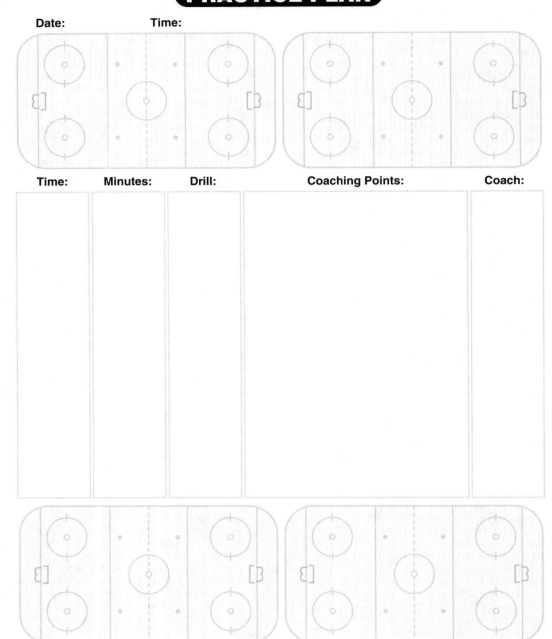

Time:	**Minutes:**	**Drill:**	**Coaching Points:**	**Coach:**

PRACTICE PLAN

Date: **Time:**

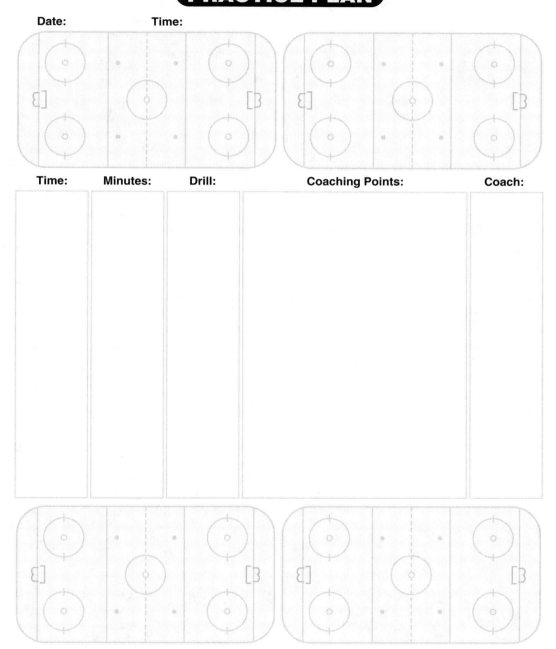

Time:	**Minutes:**	**Drill:**	**Coaching Points:**	**Coach:**

PRACTICE PLAN

Date: **Time:**

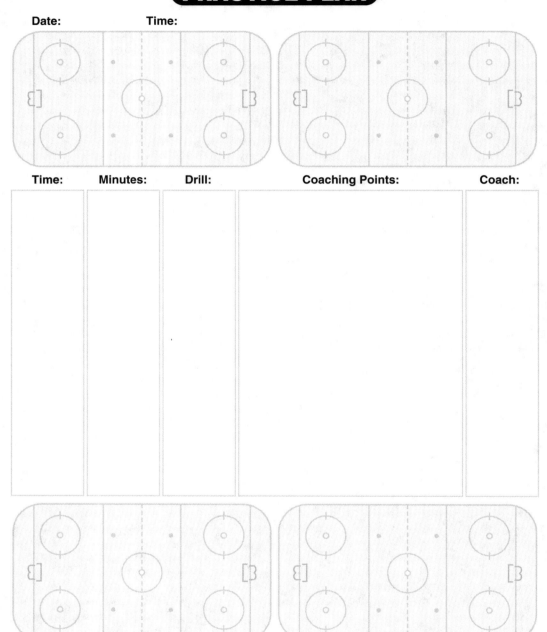

Time:	**Minutes:**	**Drill:**	**Coaching Points:**	**Coach:**

PRACTICE PLAN

Date: **Time:**

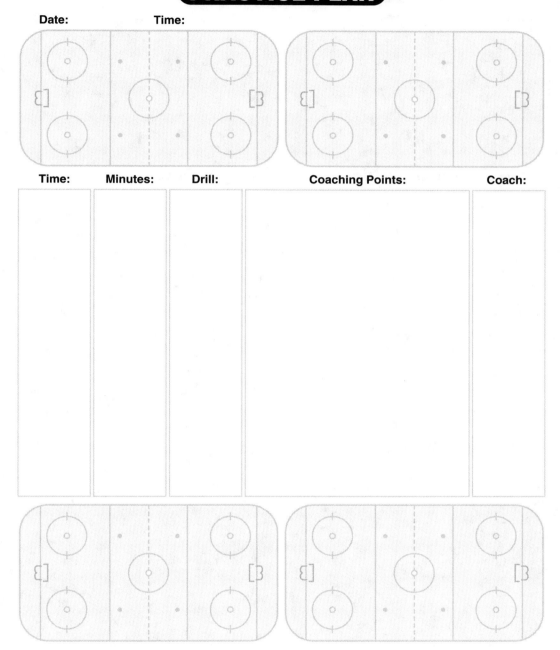

Time:	**Minutes:**	**Drill:**	**Coaching Points:**	**Coach:**

PRACTICE PLAN

Date: **Time:**

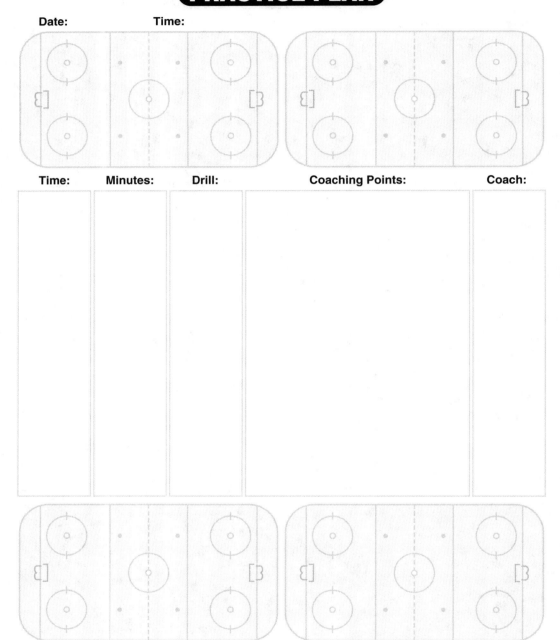

Time:	**Minutes:**	**Drill:**	**Coaching Points:**	**Coach:**

PRACTICE PLAN

Date: **Time:**

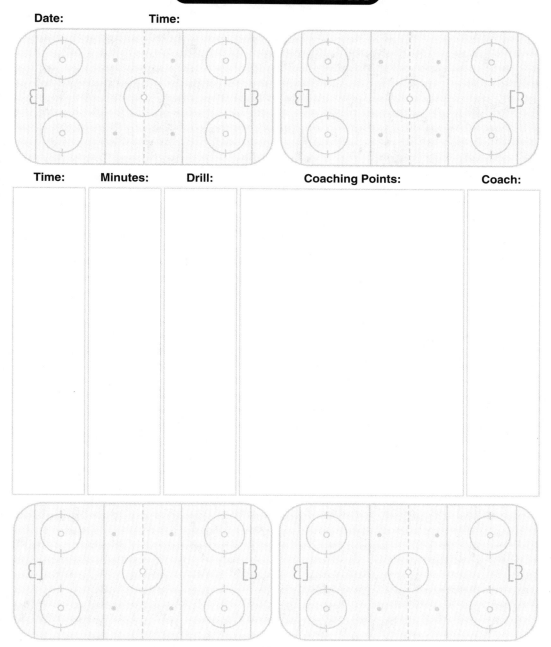

Time:	Minutes:	Drill:	Coaching Points:	Coach:

ACKNOWLEDGMENTS

I have worked with, and seen the work of, many fine ice hockey coaches over the year. This drillbook has been a compilation of not only my efforts, but theirs, too. I would like to specifically recognize several people including Tim Zimmerman, Mike Reynolds, Pete Morris, Tim Taladay, Blenn Adamo, Rob Abel, Kevin Donald, Butch Porrino, Bob Blair, Lou Manzione, Vinny Claps, Rick Handchen, Pat Doyle, Bob Auriemma, Joe Patterson, Dick Trimble, Paul Cannata, Bob Cielo, and Derek LaLonde as well as my assistant coaches at Manasquan High School, Ken Biedzynski and Craig Beattie. Also to be cited are the coaching staffs at the many summer camps I have visited over the years including Princeton University, Providence College, Cornell University, the U.S. Military Academy at West Point, the Turcotte Stickhandling School, the Ocean Hockey School, Robby Glantz Powerskating clinics, and the Laura Stamm Powerskating programs.

Since coaching through drills is essentially a science of borrowing and modifying, all of the aforementioned have been of tremendous help in my endeavors. Each of the drills in this book was taught and tested by the author in various practices so that coaching points and warning signals could be included for the reader. Some drills were designed specifically for this volume, too.

With over 450 drills, it is hoped that each coach can find something that they would like to borrow and incorporate in their own practices.

Drill 'em and work 'em hard, but always with creativity, a purpose and a smile.